GETTING AHEAD OF THE GAYME: MAN FIRST, GAY SECOND

A MATCHMAKER'S MEMOIR ON COMPATIBILITY,
BEHAVIORAL ASSESSMENT, AND INSPIRATIONAL EXPERIENCE

MASON R. GLENN

To Dann
with much love –

Mason

2/"/17

PAGE PUBLISHING, INC.
New York, NY

First originally published by Page Publishing, Inc. 2017

ISBN 978-1-63568-168-0 (Paperback)
ISBN 978-1-63568-169-7 (Digital)

Printed in the United States of America

Never love anyone who treats you like you're ordinary.

—Oscar Wilde

I remember one of my first dates, coming into my own as a gay man. I met this one eccentric man after work for coffee. During our rather succinct conversation, he asked me where my home state of Georgia was on a U.S. map. He also told me about all the "twisters" in Georgia while debating an argument on the difference between a twister and hurricane and if there was one at all.

Welcome to my life. Welcome to a gay man's dating life.

I love hearing people's life experience. I think that's why matchmaking has been such a progressive thing for my soul to absorb. I was meant to do this. This is my truth and my purpose in some way. I was meant to create some sort of community wherever this life sends me.

Matchmaking kind of found me. I was at a career crossroad in my life at one point. I was intuitive, so people would always ask me my honest opinion on things, and I guess I have a maternal way with words. I remember dipping my hand in the acting pool when I first moved out to the land of dreams we know as Los Angeles. I felt I was doing all right at it, becoming memorable to a lot of casting people, but that's a part of my life I wish to bury, and I am very okay with that. It wasn't feeding my soul. I was being told what to do and how to emote it. No, thank you. I remember arriving early at one of my last auditions for a big feature film. I think someone like Taylor Lautner was being considered for my part, and um, I had no chance. Anyway, I had a second to decompress before my audition, and I remember looking on my new smartphone at that time and came across a job listing to work with a matchmaker. I had been helping a lot of people with their online dating profiles, so I thought I had nothing to lose. Turns out, this was a legit prestigious matchmaker, and me and this one other gal got the internship, out of two hundred applicants. As they say, I guess the rest is history.

I remember growing up with Barbie dolls and GI Joes. Even at that young age, I knew I was different, even when I couldn't identify what it was. I figured that I would probably figure it out later in my life, even at age five. I grew up in a family that was dominated with very masculine men, my father bring a sports newscaster and a competitive weightlifter his entire adult life, my brother following some of those athletic desires, and here is me the "creative" one, who's in theater and does plays. I don't really remember my first interaction with someone who identified themselves as gay. Maybe in high school, surprisingly. I also was an extremely late bloomer, and when everyone was enjoying their hairy legs, I was still being mistaken as a girl on the phone. So therefore, opening myself to the sexual prism was unimaginably awkward.

I wasn't really a heavy experimenter. Sure, I had my one instance in high school that caused me to go into hiding for a long time. I remember telling my best girlfriend at that time, and it was so awkward, to say the least. I felt sex was always something I was never meant to think about or explore. I was your normal celibate, overly polite and religious Southern gentleman. I was fortunate to have many great mentors in my life to expose me to be a solid, good person. I moved to LA, and that's when I started to fully bloom and transform, internally and externally. The soil in LA allowed me to enrich my soul with nutrients I had never thought to notice.

The coming-out process is different for everyone. Trust me, there is no easy time to do it either. So waiting for the right time doesn't really help you. There are more parallels in the process for most gay men I interview. People ask me all the time, "Why don't you *do* the lesbian market?" My response? There's an algorithm and an equation to men's thought and behavioral patterns for the most part, making them more predictable. Women can be all over the place from a mathematician's point of view because they are more emotional, sensitive creatures. It's just the difference in hormone release and brain patterns. For bisexuals and the transgender community, I just don't identify as that in my true core. For me, and for most gay men, we sometimes are already feeling like we are walking on eggshells dating just men; for them to date someone that prefers both can be a bit more worrisome. Regardless, to feel like I can do an authentic job, I want to match like a gay man because I internally and externally identify as one through and through.

I've been inspired lately by all sorts of coming-out stories. It's amazing to me that there is such unity although every story seems so unique. It's in the minority to have a gay man come out of his mother's womb on a rainbow slide with a tiara on top on his newborn head. The more exceptionally accepting families usually come from very liberal parts of the nation. Because homosexuality is more into societal awareness today, the LGBT community, in general, is being better understood and accepted. I mean, look at all the conversations of gay marriage that have been occurring in recent years. However, I am rather hopeful that we can sustain the integrity of that status in the advent of our new leadership in the United States. I am lucky to be in Los Angeles, which is such a melting pot of different cultures and experiences. I feel like although we are a more liberal-minded city, the individual process and experience that we were subjected to in our growing years were heavily influenced by religion and societal norms.

The phrase "come out" really doesn't resonate with me. It seems to cheapen the decision and conversation. To do that isn't as simple as stepping through a doorway, but maybe it's more in a metaphysical sense. It's more like an action of revealing oneself in authenticity for the first time in his or her life.

What I can say is that on average, most gay men, at the latest, come out before they start a career of some kind. This is all, of course, based on my personal experience. It's also normal for gay men to identify as bisexual before they come into their own and embrace their gaydom entirely. I was in that boat for a little while. Vaginas are scary now to me. I do realize that our culture loves to compartmentalize, and yes, there is somewhat of a sliding scale in sexual attraction. Everyone has their time and story, and I often hear both. Gay men figure that they are starting a new grown-up chapter in their life, so that gives them that extra push to come out. Interviewing all ages of men, it's so crazy to me how generational differences have affected the coming-out process in general. For example, gay men over forty years of age would sometimes have to go to the one gay bar in secret in their town or meet in the park past dusk to meet people. Now, everything is so digital, which allows people to be conveniently driven to come out quicker. Individuals can explore their sexuality behind closed doors, and no one would ever know. This practice is pretty normative in the evolution of a gay man. A lot of newly gay men date or have sexual relations with the wrong people just to mess up and learn from the experiences altogether. Once they've solidified or have a clearer direction in where they want to go, that's when they become more independent in their sexuality, where it doesn't matter anymore what people think. One goes from being an easily swayed boy to a more grounded man.

On the flip side, these types of men that can be erratic in their gay careers, or men who have had previous heterosexual relationships, sometimes with children even, and now have discovered themselves authentically and now identify themselves as homosexual. I like that our current generation is beginning to be more understanding that two mommies or daddies is okay. The alienation is becoming less and less, and it's inspiring to see the progression itself. There is a lot of judgment based on men who are late bloomers. Everyone has a time and reason for how they come out, so what makes your process better than his that you feel he should do? What I will say is that on average, men who are out all the way do not want to date someone who is not completely out. Meaning, they don't want to date someone whom they feel like they can't hold their hand in public. I get it. Of course, I have met men that don't even care. In retrospect, parents not knowing is normally okay, but when the person you are dating feels like a secret, that's when that conversation can approach a solid roadblock.

As you can imagine though, newly gay men can have many high expectations, but these expectations slowly dwindle as a gay man matures. Imagine what would happen if you had a couple of moral expectations and personal preferences when you are young, and imagine how much dating experience you would have had in the long-term. On average, I have met a lot of younger men with a laundry list of things at times, then I'll interview a man who's over forty that only has a couple of things. I understand that some of these men come from different generational time periods, but also, there are men who came out decades apart from each other, so sometimes that doesn't even alter my presumption of the equation.

Once you become this new man, be cognizant that you are surrounding yourself with gay men that are great influences to you and hold you accountable to bad character choices. By surrounding yourself with men that inspire you to be a better man, it's always setting you up for positive, more attractive character absorption for potential mates.

I remember coming across an article about Williams syndrome. Watching these men and women was something that was inspirationally magnanimous. The diagnosed experienced a number of health issues, but mostly they were characterized with the gift of instantaneous love and trust to anyone, an apparent affability, even to complete strangers. A normal person would keep his or her distance when a stranger would bang their knee on a table. However, a person with Williams syndrome would go to their immediate aide and offer help. I felt like I, coming from a small town in Georgia to such a big city, would offer a sense of cordial generosity, but I found myself having to adjust in the other direction. Los Angeles is notorious for having the ideal of "how little can I give you but get the most return out of you." Believe me, I found my squad that is very generous. Over time, I found that I had to hinder myself, that "Yes, ma'am" no longer was a term of endearment but now was insulting to someone's age. Sometimes I think we as humans are the ones with the illness, and the people with Williams syndrome are the normal ones.

Follow my journey of how you can inspire yourself to be a better person and lover. Sometimes we as humans can be content as exactly as we are based on all the homogenous atmosphere that surrounds us. Sometimes, though, creating a relationship with someone can shake up that idealism, create growth, and positive change. Whether it be via my truth or some compatibility assessments I have learned over the years, we are our own GPS that redirects us when we make a good or bad choice. However, in the end, we always end up on the destination on where we are supposed to be and with whom will accompany us in that journey along the way. Maybe this is my spiritual side speaking, but most things happen for a reason, and the universe works its magic in its mysterious ways. The conversations and experiences we encounter through companionship in all its facets shape our thought processes for the better, whether we label it as a success or failure. You might laugh, you might cry, and then again you might disagree on some things. In the end, there'll be a certain change, I hope, and that is my source of trying to become a beacon to create a colorful future for those who read my story.

Nostalgia

I had the great pleasure of interviewing my grandmother about her secret to long-lived happiness with a partner. She is a true Southern belle, loves her garden, bowling league on Wednesdays, and she always gets her hair done on Thursdays. She is in her mid-eighties now, my only grandparent left to date. Sixty-five years of dedicated marriage. Wow, so inspiring, right? That woman has an inspiring story of true love I wish to share. She and my grandfather would always say, "That's a winner." In life, I always want to win for myself more than anything else, and that's enough.

I grew up going to my grandparents' houses pretty much every other weekend. We did the simplest things in life, which enriched my soul exponentially. We'd go fishing, pick blackberries to make jam that day, or go to the church playground. I would ride my electronic Jeep, and my older brother would ride his go-cart in a field where my grandparents would always have tomato, squash, and muscadine vines adorning the fresh earth. We would play Monopoly and card games and would watch *Wheel of Fortune* together at night. We would always eat together, something I never really did growing up with my actual family. I joke that my mother found the microwave and never looked back. This kind of changed her presumed role as a fabulous Southern cook. Stouffer's lasagna or Lipton butter noodles were always a dinner favorite. "What's for dinner?" I would ask, and the response was "Whatever is in the freezer." Although, my mother always made the best waffles in that old-school waffle iron as I watched Saturday morning cartoons. With my grandparents especially, we were always building a sense of community. I am so very thankful I had these positive representations of strong character in front of me for most of my adult life thus far.

My grandmother first saw my grandfather when she was twelve years old. She told me, "I'll always remember him in those overalls and plaid shirt on the dirt basketball court. He had the biggest brown eyes." I love this start because she realized that there was *something* about this man, even before she barely knew him. That woman had intuition I think we can all learn from. Years passed, and she finally saw him again "scooping ice cream at the corner store." Sometimes fate has a way with us and has a strong sense of humor. Some time elapsed, and then she found herself on a double date with him, but he had his own date already. Before they knew it, they had "locked eyes" on that nondate date. They broke up with their significant others abruptly, and they started dating each other. Obviously, keep in mind this is years ago in a very small rural town. By no means is this really recommended in today's age, but it seemed a lot more innocent then.

I remember riding in the car to see my new nephew, and my grandmother recalled a story of how she was sixteen years old getting on a Greyhound bus to Atlanta to get a job. She didn't know what she was applying for, but wanted to get a job at Sears off Ponce de Leon in Atlanta. She went in on a Friday, the recruiter found her a place to live, and she was called into work on a Monday. When she told my grandfather, he stated, "You've got to marry me. If you go to Atlanta, you'll find someone else." They were married a month later. With papers in hand, my grandfather asked Mary Lou, my grandmother's mother, if they could get married. Mary Lou passed her blessing but told them if they ever fussed, she would "turn them over her checkered apron and spank both of them." My grandmother always said that if things didn't work out, "Big Momma would get rid of me and keep him." My great-grandmother loved my grandfather so much. Both my grandparents got married in a living room with a preacher as the officiant and his daughter as a witness. "He told me a hundred times he loved me," my grandmother concluded. I remember her telling me at one point that they were fairly poor, only $500 between the two of them, and moved around multiple times, but it didn't matter because they were doing and learning about life and its tumultuous rhythm together.

Devotion makes the heart grow close, and my grandmother knew this in the deepest level of connection imaginable. My grandfather was devoted to that woman with everything he had: his financial means, his emotional and physical bond, and his frequency to my grandmother's love language. Toward the end of his life, even in bad health, he would look over at her and just say, "You're beautiful." Such a powerful thing for a man to say to his loved one. I asked my grandmother what made their relationship so good, their secret. She said, "You just gotta love and respect one another." My grandfather had the best sense of humor too. He would often joke with telemarketers that asked for my grandmother to hold on because she was on the roof cleaning out the gutters, when she was standing right there next to him. He was also such a caring man.

"Let me take you to the mall and pick you up something new."

"I don't need anything new, I got enough clothes."

"Well, you should give those away so you can buy yourself new ones."

Courtship. Chivalry. Selflessness. All those things made this relationship perpetuate into a snowball of an unconditional experience. My grandmother recounted an experience a couple years ago about a man that professed his love to her as she was walking out of the local dollar store. "He said he had always loved me, but said that he knew of my grandfather and said I couldn't have married a better man." That is something I learned from him as my mentor: always be good to people and do things for people without definitive expectations. My grandmother has never pumped gas a day in her life; she now has the young boy at the local station to do it for her. My grandfather did little things like that, which said, "I love you." He married his best friend, his partner in crime, which is so much more powerful to establish especially in the beginning of a relationship.

My grandmother added, "Papa said dishes is the easiest job I had ever had." They didn't own a dishwasher ever. "Papa would wash them most of the time, and I would dry and put things up." I think this act just allowed them to do something monotonous together and to mainly focus on each other. It's quite easy for our lives to become so cumbersome with schedules and balancing our time. I like that doing something so overlooked could force them to connect in an endearing and loving way on a daily basis. It was like having it as a priority without any type of association of stress.

My grandfather was an avid smoker, but when my older brother was a very young child, he was sitting on the front steps with him and asked him, "Papa, why do you smoke?" From that day forward, he stopped, cold turkey. Everything was literally that easy to him, which is how relationships should be. Sure, there is a give and take, but the transition shouldn't be difficult, seeing every conversation as an opportunity to make you appear more attractive to your lover. It's not about a threat of changing who you are, a defamation of character, but allowing you to make minor tweaks in yourself to make your partner see your character clearer. How can I allow myself to become better for my partner? See the difference: selfishness versus selflessness.

I also never saw my grandfather ever argue or raise his voice to anyone, not even his wife. I did make my grandmother cry a couple of times when I was young, because I could be quite the spoiled pest. I definitely learned my lesson. It's almost like I set the family pet on fire. If anything, I learned that I was the selfish one, and she was only crying because she thought I had the capacity to be a good little boy. My grandma has always had such a caring and generous nature about her. She would hide money in my suitcase through the years when I would stay with them and always wanted me to feel safe and welcomed. She would always preface that she would always give "everyone the same amount" because she loved everyone the same. When my grandfather died, she gave me all his very stylish shoes. Some of my favorite boots I have worn for years and always get compliments on are these rich brown ankle boots. She'll even reshine them or the others for me when I see her. I find this almost to be like a metaphor of how Jesus would wash the feet of others. Whether you deem yourself as spiritual or not, the ideal of humility and kindness would resonate through my soul when she would do something like this. It seemed like she was put on this earth to ensure that everyone felt okay. I sometimes feel I have that same purpose in my life to some extent. It's a very Southern tradition to bring food over to friends and family that were going through troubling moments of grief, and she was no different. Every week, she would always tell me what cake or pie she made for someone because "it was their favorite." This is what is missing in a lot of relationships nowadays: serving your significant other and wanting nothing in return. I have adopted that mentality over the years. Sometimes a way to a man's heart is through his stomach. Doing things for your lover should be for you and not for them. The more you love serving your significant other, the more desire builds and positively escalates, and then things naturally come back to you.

Take it from my grandmother to have hope in this dating sea of tribulation. Sweet moments like this exist; sometimes all it takes is a certain look on a dirt basketball court and maybe even a freshly baked cake or pie.

Dec 31, 2013

Dear Macon,

It was good to have you home for Christmas.

Looking forward to seeing you again in the spring.

If you like coconut pie you can use this same recipe, just omit the Cocoa and pecans and add a small can of coconut. It's good.

I won $750 dollars in a coconut pie contest. Its call french coconut pie.

I hope everything goes good with your new job.

Love you so much,

Mama Sue

Chocolate Pecan Pie

3 beaten eggs
1½ cups sugar
1 tablespoon plain flour (all purpose)
¼ cup buttermilk
1 stick butter or Margarine (melted)
¼ teaspoon salt
1 teaspoon Vanilla
3 tablespoons Hersheys Cocoa
1 cup chopped pecans

Cream eggs and sugar together, add other ingredients and Mix Well. Pour into a deep 9 inch (thawed) pie crust. Bake about 1 hr. at 325°. Put it on a baking sheet to bake. When the crust begins to brown a little, make a ring out of foil and cover crust so it won't get brown. If you don't have butter milk, add lemon juice to sweet milk until it gets thick.

14

Is in Italian

I remember downloading a popular dating application for only the second time in my life, really not having any expectations. It's the one that feels much dirtier now than it used to be. I feel like the first time I downloaded the application was for the sole purpose of fooling around with other men, not knowing what the heck I was doing. I was definitely in the "pretend I am an expert" mode, but honestly was utilizing my encounters for the purpose of formulating how to love in that way as a gay man physically. It was quite scary, but I took the necessary leap.

I'll always remember one of my first experiences was meeting this guy in his mansion right in the hills of Silverlake, a neighboring hipster town. You know, the kind of house that echoed. He told me I should be a porn star, which I found weird. He also was a Hollywood producer that would fan off famous people he knew, and I was snoring in my head. One of my sluttiest moments was when a torrential windstorm dominated LA years ago one October. I remember all of these events happening around the same time. I didn't have power or hot water for a solid week, and my place at that time remained fifty degrees. So I thought it would be a great idea to sleep with someone different every night for four days to have a warm shower and bed each night. This wasn't one of my proudest moments, but this really confirmed my ability of manipulation, something a therapist of mine has told me I should be aware of. I saw this man two or three more times, but that was the first time I realized that I was nothing more than his play toy. He'd play with me then put me back in his toy box, while I remained in darkness, waiting for him to play with me again. At that point, I realized that this idea of casual sex can put a toll on a human being's mental stability whether we elicit certain behaviors or not.

Anyway, so here I am years later, using this application again, maybe as an opportunity to find dates. I met up with a hot Asian mom and "her gays" because I was single and needed to not be such a grandpa all the time. The couple that went with us said they had met on this same dating application, which gave me a little hope to utilize it for maybe a coffee date or two. I got on and saw this guy, and it seemed like he took his profile picture at Coachella, a very popular outdoor music festival. I liked what he wrote, and we were messaging casually. I could tell he was interested in me, so it wasn't very long until both of us met at a Starbucks to get to know each other more. I, at that time, was working on myself, and when he arrived, I was buried in one of my self-help books. I secretly was reading it to make me look smarter. I have no idea why I did that. I don't think he even knows my secret today.

It wasn't long until we were dating, and on our second date, he came by my place and dropped off some half-opened bottles of wine. He worked for a wine company, and he seemed to be really busy, and it stood out to me that he took some time out of the chaos of his day to see me.

It wasn't long before we were intimate for the first time, nothing too crazy. I think he got really comfortable with me and started lacking on the gentlemanly qualities that I was looking for in an ideal mate. He was late multiple times for our dates. Not just the LA-fifteen-minutes late, but the half-hour-to-an-hour late: bad first impression central. Seriously, manage your time like an adult. I told him if he was late one more time, I wouldn't answer him anymore. Being "busy" wasn't an excuse if it was a noticeable pattern. He listened to me and started being more punctual. I was also impressed that he stopped putting our relationship on blast via social media. I wouldn't say I am pretentiously private, but it got to the point where I would find out things first from social media rather than him telling me in person. He stopped that real quickly. I thought to myself, *Wow, instead of falling through the cracks, he patched them.* It left me with even more of a desire to start liking him and this may be turning into *love.* I hadn't been in love before with another man, but this felt different, in a good way. So maybe I did get a glimpse of it, and being the hopeless romantic I thought I was at that time, I was beginning to let my guard down.

A month or so passed, and I remember being in the car, heading to my best friend's karaoke birthday. I remember saying to him, "So are we boyfriends now or what?" We had a giggle, and that was when we decided to be official.

There was something so special about this man. He had such a heart and such a passionate way of looking at life. That was what attracted me to him. I was naive, so believe me, I wasn't perfect and hated speaking my feelings. Six months of therapy helped me with that at a later time. It's so weird that I can speak my thoughts clearly in a business environment. We all have points in our personality that make us feel uncomfortably vulnerable.

We spent a lovely weekend in wine country. We went on a trip to San Diego together. His affluent best friend also took us—well, me—to see my gay idol, Shania Twain. Front row seats. Insert gay-man high-pitched squeal here. I will be forever grateful to his friend, who has always been so kind and generous to me. I even got to be on stage with her and sing harmonies. I died. Be jealous.

Relationships always go in stages, and I was approaching that point in our relationship where some of his behaviors seemed very selfish, narcissistic, and without consideration of us creating a future together. Things like that had become more prevalent. Toward the very end of our relationship, everything escalated more in deciding where we were moving. He had a beautiful cat, which I loved dearly and would play with when I would see him. The problem was that I had been blood tested for allergies, and cat dander/hair was in the red zone for me. One of the other matchmakers in our office made a social media post that I thought was really funny. She talked about three ways to instantly become more attractive to potential mates. One was to stop smoking, one was to shave your beard, and the other was to get rid of your cat. Anyway, I didn't really complain about his cat, but I felt that I was giving up a lot already and didn't understand why he wouldn't budge on some things. I essentially would have this whole routine of changing pillowcases, taking a pill, lint-rolling the sheets—it was what it was. He then told me that I was telling him where to live, which I honestly had a compromising conversation on that I didn't want to spend double my rent when he was the one who wanted a two-bedroom apartment, with a balcony, because *his* cat must have room. The idea was for me to save money, but it was hard for me to budge when the price of my rent was a steal, living on my own.

I really liked this guy; I was willing to do what it took to keep him. We are only willing to accept the love we put out, right? I asked, what was he doing for me? He would complain about never having enough money, and even after he told me that he was making almost six figures. I remember a time when he went with me to a friend's birthday and bought all these bakery items for everyone, when we really could have bought a $10 cake at a local supermarket. I told him that "I would rather us go to Del Taco and spend $10 on a meal for the both of us" if we were going cheap. I had a feeling he blamed me for making him spend money. Dude, you are an adult, no one is pressuring you to do anything, nor have I even had an expectation. I think there were a couple of times where he felt he had to pay for me because the dinner was well over $200. I felt bad for not wanting to pay for something like that, unless the occasion called for it. I am from the South, where I grew up on cheap, processed food. For me to spend more than $20 on a meal for the most part is just plain silly. Do you see a pattern? He would find a way to make him look like a victim rather than the source of an issue, just another narcissistic behavior that would fester. He did tell me, "When you make more money, your demand on life goes up." I never knew what he meant by that. I think it meant that he felt the need to keep up with the Joneses. I, however, am fine with my studio apartment whether I am making a huge income or not. I live simplistically, and I am fine with this.

In my breakup e-mail, I told him, "The thing that scares me the most is I am open to exploring a more solidified future with you, but I hear a lot of 'I' in conversation about *your* future, when I've been saying 'we' and 'our' all this time. You say '*I* need a child to carry *my* heritage,' '*I* need to be financially stable,' '*I* need to be comfortable,' '*I* need a house by this area.' Consistently talking in first person makes me feel that I am forced to agree with you or that I am not a part of a long-term plan with you. Having personal goals are great, but I see a distinct difference in the amount of first person you say versus the latter. Even when I bring these things up, especially children, you don't want to budge and can be quite combative, whether you realize this or not. I know your goals very distinctly, but thinking back, I don't think you know mine. Sometimes you want to get to all these personal goals done, but you are so focused on exactly how you want it to be that I in turn can feel neglected and forgotten. If you want to do those things exactly as you want them, it will be better if you were single." I'll always remember us being at a party and him telling his friends about how he wanted a kid *his* way, while I felt like I was the shunned kid in time-out.

Now that years have passed since us breaking up, I have started seeing the signs of a true narcissist. It's funny, I went to a psychic and a numerologist after our breakup, and they both said, "I don't like him. He is a very selfish man."

How we broke up was, well, juicy for you to read. I sent him another e-mail after he was very distant and stressed because of work one day. He hadn't texted me all day but made time to meet his friends after work when he knew I needed to talk to him. That didn't sit well with me. I honestly felt he put himself in a high state of stress all the time. Maybe I was too carefree. Anyway, I sat him down on a Tuesday and told him most of these things I had mentioned prior. I sent him an e-mail the next day, trying to be more eloquent, and he sent me his response the next day ending with, "I woke up very upset this morning, and I need this weekend to breathe a little. Unless you have already made up your mind, I would prefer to talk on Monday night. However, if you have made up your mind, I want to know ASAP." Then, the next day, I found out from social media that he was out of town. His main girlfriend called me first thing on that Friday morning saying, "What the fuck is going on?" Great way to start my day. I honestly didn't see her as being nosey. She was a great influence on him, and I later thanked her for that, even though she never really talked to me again. Oh well, some things are just what they are through a divorce. Maybe my expectations are too high for him.

She did say, "I am really happy that he has met you. You guys go well together," or something to that extent. I asked to meet her for coffee the next day. By no means did I want to seem as a martyr; I was just being honest and knew some things could have been my fault too.

I remember that Saturday morning at our neighborhood coffee shop and her looking me in the eye and saying, "He is in Miami, and he asked if you were okay." I remember keeping my composure, but my heart sunk to the deepest parts of the darkest depth of any ocean. I thought to myself, *Why is he in Miami? He hasn't mentioned being there before.* Earlier on, when we agreed to "take a break" that previous night, I told him there would be not as much communication and no physical anything, to help us create some space. I found out later that he took that as we had broken up completely for some reason. So he fled. I never knew what truly went down that weekend. I spent that Saturday in what probably was a panic attack, and my friends were like "Where is he?" I knew that "I don't know" was a truly embarrassing answer. I remember walking for hours. I couldn't be stagnant and still. I had to keep moving to feel like I could survive. Later he informed me he spent some time with some old guys that weekend and just lounged by the pool, clearing his head. I do think that was exactly what he did, but then again, with me feeling "so betrayed and embarrassed," as my psychologist later put it, I don't know if I could have given myself the opportunity to believe him without giving myself the opportunity to escape. One of my friends who was a native also told me that the largest gay circuit party was there the weekend he went. Oh boy.

I sent him a text Sunday evening as I was walking to meet a friend for coffee, and he said for us to meet the next day, as planned. It's funny how we opened and then closed our doors at that same Starbucks. Side note: I was editing this chapter in my book at the same ground zero. Oh, universe. After grabbing my chai, he sat me down, looked at me, smiled slightly, and said, "Yunno, we're just not right for each other." Keep in mind, he only knew that I read his last e-mail, and that was where we last left each other. I sat there stone-cold. I'll always remember his smirk. I honestly don't remember what I said. I'm sure I had given up at this point, and it didn't matter.

After he was done, I remember mentioning to him that I knew he was in Miami. He stood up and yelled, "How could she do this to me? All I wanted to tell you is what happened this weekend." Then, he stormed off.

I walked to his car, adrenaline pumping. All I wanted to know was what happened in Miami. If this man cheated on me, I deserved to know, after a year of being with him. He then screamed at me in the parking lot, saying, "After all I've done *for her*!" I felt like there was a giant neon sign right above me, as the patrons looked on to the commotion we were causing. He then drove off. I texted him, saying, "I deserve closure. That's all I was going to ask. What happened this weekend you wanted to tell me? I don't understand why you think I betrayed you. I've done nothing malicious." Three minutes later, he wrote back, "I am in front of your place. I am sorry, I am so angry. I love you, and my heart is broken. And she just hurt me so bad. I just want to give you a hug and be on my way." He was mad at his friend telling me where he was. Wasn't he the one who asked her to see if I was okay? At this point, I got back to my place after getting some gas. I sat in his car and just started bawling. Crying so hard that I could barely breathe. All I wanted was for him to take ownership. So I had to find a way to figure out how to give myself closure. I gave him a hug, we exchanged keys, and I told him, "Thank you for showing me what love was in the most sincere way," and that I would never villainize him. I still stand by those statements, even today.

The next morning, my phone was blowing up, and I accidentally texted him, saying, "He and I are over, but it is for the best." He responded, "Was this supposed to be for me?" then I succinctly told him my world was turned upside-down and that it was a mere accident. He apologized again, and then we didn't talk for a while.

A week or two passed, and he sent me an e-mail that disclosed that our mutual friend was diagnosed with a progressed stage of cancer, with her treatment details, and he also said something along the lines of "As we both process our breakup, I hope we can become friends one day." I sent him a reply that basically said, "You don't even know what you did wrong, and for that reason, I don't want to be your friend." Sorry, "friends" don't do shitty things like that to someone without apologizing. I think for a long time, as much as I wanted full closure, I told my psychologist that I felt he owed me an apology, and it wasn't my job to tell him. The thing about narcissists is that humility is their kryptonite.

I saw him again a month later for the first time, and I could tell he was trying to talk to me. Sorry, pal, I don't want to talk to you. Funny thing, at my birthday months later, he was trying to convince a close friend of mine via text that I was villainizing him. I found this out eventually after he had "aimlessly tried to call, text, and e-mail me," and I didn't respond to him. I handed my phone over, and my friend clearly saw that there were no texts, calls, or e-mails he was referring to. I won't even get into the other things that he did that made his ditch seem like an endless black hole. The thing is, is that he just made himself look even worse. His actions spoke louder than my words. I learned to not partake in the negative too much. I would be doing nothing by creating more gossip. Seems like I let people develop their own opinions about him, and I didn't have to do anything to make him look bad. I am still friends with a lot of his friends, but mine don't want to have anything to do with him. I had conversations with his friends, saying, "He doesn't have friends that hold him accountable for some of his behaviors." I want my friends to tell me I am being a prissy bitch or a complete dick. I felt his friends would just smile and nod at him and sometimes chime in to his sexual adventures. Months passed, and from there, we started checking in with each other. He is happy for me, and I am happy for him. I actually tried to set him up on a friend date. He doesn't know that I referred him to some anonymous business even after our breakup. I think holding myself to a higher standard in regard to integrity places me in a better space. I don't need to brag; I want to be able to stand proud by my own standards. By no means do I think this man is evil or that I am near perfect. I just feel he wasn't looking for an opportunity to fall in love, even to this day. He has recently told me that he has found his husband, but his heartthrob won't be ready for another two years. This guy seemed like a model to me, and this was intertwined in a conversation of him talking about all the guys he was meeting on mobile dating applications. For me, one must reach a feeling of equilibrium, and that's when the laws of attraction start billowing. I hope he has found it or will find it soon, but it isn't my responsibility to take care of him, as much as I feel I would be a good influence on him. I know he's probably reached a better point in his life in some way, but I don't know if I will care to know that in depth anymore.

This man was my first true love, and we went through a lot, but in doing that, I realized that I refuse to not be willing to speak my mind. It made me be mindful of falling in love with someone's potential rather than their actuality. Time to wear my big boy pants, iron a couple of shirts, and polish my shoes while I am at it. Sometimes, I explored what it would be like to get my shoes dirty. I really was able to give myself permission to feel the permanence of sexual desire as a gay man. Being vocal about being sexual was no longer as intimidating. I didn't have to play a prudish part anymore. All I have for this man is gratitude for allowing me to be a better version of me. "My dearest Mason, you bring so much happiness to my life and continue to remind me that there are still genuine, kind-hearted people in this world. It is not difficult to love you or be there for you, and I hope your day is filled with as much love as you put out into the world. Have a great day!" That is what the definition of authentic love is and how it can transform you to love again. Thank you.

Dirty Laundry:
Sex and Relationships

"I am only a bottom. I find that I cannot date a versatile guy." I hear these accounts from time to time. In today's age, we are becoming less accustomed to sexual roles and desire to create more lasting moments. I actually don't get a lot of stark sexual preferences as much as I used to. I get it, though; sexual chemistry is important to a lot of us gay dudes. Sometimes I feel I am asexual, so my need to have consistent sex has never been on the top of my list. Do you like to have a penis up your butt all the time? Well, some of us don't want it either, but we find pleasure in it anyway. I swear I had dated five men back-to-back that either had erectile dysfunction because of alcohol, medication, or just pure delayed anatomical response. Then at another point, I felt for the longest time it was a me thing, that I was meant to lie on my back and be a bottom for the rest of my life. When it comes to it, for me, I don't like being subjected to a norm and having a role. I like to know that the discovery of sexual exploration is invigorating, exciting, and random. I don't like feeling like there is an ordinary outline that I must follow every time my partner and I decide to get frisky. Therefore, I am 100 percent versatile. Maybe I just haven't experienced a relationship where I was subjected with a role label and found it different and continuously enjoyable. Overall, I have seen relationships be more successful in this preference. I get it; sexual compatibility is very key to some gay men. Some men just won't budge, but keep in mind, you just cut your search by a big chunk. It's just one piece of the relationship puzzle at the end of the day.

I receive an abundance of inquires on dating advice about writing about sex, and honestly, there's not much to write about. Does sexual position matter? What happens if you meet someone who has the same sexual preference position as you? If you are looking to hook up, of course, do you for instant gratification. If you are in a loving, monogamous relationship, it should not matter, in my humble opinion. Was that too blatant for you? Good, it should be. If you like someone enough, you'll figure it out. Once you start seeing your partner as a part of you, you stop seeing the relationship as a set of presumed roles, but as a moldable partnership that is ever changing. Do things for your partner because they enjoy them, whether that is sex or not. A little selflessness goes a long way in the gay world, and for it to be a deal breaker is absurd.

I see sexual position preference as something you might crave for indulgence, like a brownie a la mode. Once you have it, you are satisfied, until you get that craving again, regardless of frequency. Some people like whipped cream on their brownie, and some like chocolate sauce, and others without a cherry. Have I made enough sexual innuendo references for you, or are you still with me? When you are in a committed relationship, think of your favorite dessert as a buffet. Some days you might want pecans on top, and some days you might want mint chocolate ice cream instead of your normal vanilla bean flavor. Doesn't having options sound so much more attractive than a forced choice with no substitutions? With the right chemistry, anything can happen, and anything is possible. You're welcome.

We gay men are more judgmental sometimes to one another, in our own community, rather than on the individuals on the outside. The topic of open relationships gave me this inclination. There was little gray area on this topic for a majority in this informal panel discussion I led. You were either for or against it. There wasn't any of the talk of the "given a certain circumstance" gray area.

"It isn't a relationship if it's open." This was in response to someone who was against the idea of open relationships, and the argument was that "people like this are the reason people heavily stereotype the LGBT community." The response was "Disagree. You're thinking of promiscuity, not an open relationship. People in an open relationship share a good deal of communication, negotiation, and discussion about what their partner is and is not okay with." But even in the straight world, open relationships are still considered unconventional and taboo to most. Hence, the promiscuity label is on both ends of the sexual orientation spectrum. A lot of people would say that open or polyamorous relationships are quite stigmatized. Not all open relationships exist in Utah.

"Lies and deceit are not symptoms of open relationships. Lies and deceit are symptoms of weak relationships." I then go into saying what defines a relationship as "weak," and if it were that, why would a person still be with the other? For me, I base everything mostly on evidence of similar dialogue and statistics drawn from my intake interviews. Maybe my control group is a bit biased, but I will say, the evidence comes from data of past dating experience and involvement in this topic, not people's current status. Unfortunately, a vast majority of the men I have interviewed that have experienced an open relationship experienced some type of personal malice. A person told me that the love of his life for years wanted to open things up, and then he fell in love with the third person and left him; this was enough for me to have my own opinion about the issue itself. I just have too much heart, and that will always be my personal weakness. To each his own, though. All the men we have worked with enjoy knowing that we only work with monogamous men, and this is a safe haven for them. Polyamorous men are looking for more sexual exploration, because they feel they have the foundation of emotional attachment with their committed partner. They need a formulation of consistent spontaneity and freedom to explore sexuality. These men can have the viewpoint of feeling like we as a gay community have been shamed so much, so why not explore all facets of sexuality and the invigoration it can present. To me, the gay community is already so shamed for being too sexual, uncommitted, and drug-induced. We are considered "dirty" to a lot of people, but it is interesting that monogamous men sometimes view polyamorous men as dirty within the parameters of our own community. These men would have better luck finding this on a mobile dating application that is geared more to those sexual desires. Speaking of, I have no desire to go on a naked camping trip with a whole bunch of other horny gay dudes. I have a problem with someone wanting to go naked to a spa. That does not sound fun—at all. I think polyamorous men would argue that it would be freeing and cathartic. We are just wired differently, and we can agree to disagree.

My inquisitive nature sometimes gets the very best of me. I remember meeting this one guy who was in a committed relationship for over a decade. We had been chatting for what seemed to be six months or so, very passively. He said around the eight-year mark, his Cuban and jealous nature almost destroyed his relationship. Both he and his partner decided to open it so both could see other men on the side, alleviating that jealous nature, making everything seem more even. That allegedly saved their relationship. It's funny how a jealous issue could still be seen as a jealous issue, but for some reason, it worked for them. I felt so strange seeing him, and apparently, they don't get to know the same guy together, but see random others on the side. I remember him telling me they don't "usually play with the same guy apart." For me, I had a big problem with the label of him having an open relationship, because that led to the impression that he wanted to be intimate with other people, and then he was intimate with his committed partner, who also was being intimate with others. Those tally marks were too much out of my comfort zone. He was very well versed in being sexually healthy, but that wave of truth was something I didn't wish to ride, figuratively speaking.

On another account, I remember meeting this younger couple on a more grungy dating application. I dismissed them because the communication was very staggered with them. They had the same position preference. I mean their screen name was something like TwoTopMen. I can only assume so much at this point. I didn't think much of it, though. They seemed like solid guys, so we were casually chatting, all three of us. I was so intrigued by their dynamic. They viewed dating someone else as like regular dating: one entity dating another. I guess that made sense for me in the short-term. After all, I don't like to judge things unless I experience them myself. Both guys were polar opposites, one very artistic, and the other a very intelligent researcher in the science realm. We wound up watching cheesy old horror movies one night together, making pozole at

3:00 a.m., and talking about chemical receptors in the brain stem. I remember lying on the couch as we were watching one film, and one of them started rubbing my foot, then the other guy came over and sandwiched me in. We went upstairs, and I was in the middle. I felt like Dracula with my hands across my shoulders. So as we got comfortable, we all started kissing and fooling around, but nothing too crazy. What that experience made me realize is that I am not meant to be polyamorous. In my recollection, I was telling myself to constantly be "even," making sure one guy felt like he was getting attention just as much as the other. As the third, I felt it was my duty to consistently check in, and that seemed unnatural and impeded the flow of natural connection. Maybe this was a fault of mine and an unsolicited responsibility I had because I wanted the context of the relationship to be fair. My brain couldn't wrap itself around the idea of being comfortable with touching someone intimately when his partner of some years was right next to me. They said they wouldn't be doing this if their relationship wasn't strong, but there was this cinematic moment where I felt something was a bit off. There is no way in hell I could ever see my partner being touched by another man when we have expressed the word *love* to each other. Honestly, it seemed that this was merely a thrilling novelty to me. I was so thankful for this experience because it reaffirmed my understanding of this ideal in our community and solidified why monogamy works for me.

In one theory of mine, I see this traditional viewpoint has to do with factors of relationship mentorship, growing up in a divorced home, as well as other sociographic factors. Over time, I've also noticed that gay men who have experienced infidelity often revert to more of an open lifestyle as well. It would be interesting to study these correlations further—maybe in my next book. I also read an account where the idea of open relationships is increasing with the rise of the millennial generation. The idea of polyamory can be a conflicting ideal to someone's relationship identity, and that may be a deal breaker. "We are just following society's guidelines of what we 'should or shouldn't do,'" someone said in support of open relationships.

I've met some guys where it works somehow, as I don't want to veer too far from the idea of an open relationship. "Men are biologically wired to physically mate with as many as possible. This is why I think open relationships work for some. They can compartmentalize and separate their emotional bonds from their sexual liaisons," another person mentioned in the discussion. I did appreciate the mammal and specie-centric view, saying that a lot of species are meant to have multiple partners. Keep in mind, we shouldn't compare an ape with a human, on many levels. Apes do not have cell phones, careers, obligations, and mental advancements that we have as a human race. Mammals have one purpose usually, and that is to mate, for the most part. If that were my sole purpose in life, of course I would have multiple partners! To compare them, to me, isn't fair or equal. If we view history as a full spectrum, I do see that monogamy is very new to our current world. Sometimes we battle innate process versus what is seen as conventionally and current as defined by society: the argument of biological nature versus social nurture.

I remember seeing one account saying, "I found the love of my life, but still had the desire to be with somebody else." This same person also mentions closeted gay men and how they are forced to be monogamous, but start being polyamorous in the experimental phase. Does monogamy come natural to you or does it sometimes feel like a sacrifice?

"My husband and I have been together for nearly thirty-one years. We were each other's first lovers and remain committed to this day. Our definition of commitment may vary from that of other couples, but we were totally monogamous for three years, created a solid foundation, and now have been open/polyamorous since 1988. I have a partner of eight years, and over the years, we have extended ourselves into an extended family that contains within it many different levels of partnerships. It is a grand life. My husband and I remain physically intimate, and we encourage, welcome, and support other like-minded men to chat with us anytime." I find that men who only see the same person or people together, formulating some sort of mutually understood pattern, have more success. Even reading this, I get why it works for them, but there are too many variables that would make me uncomfortable, and I think a lot of other monog-amous guys would feel the same way. Open relationships are very intimidating and unnatural to us monogamous men. I can say that I did notice more openness among the older generation of gay men. My take is that most men of today's age would be too jealous to have that happen or would just agree to call it quits and move on if it got to that point. Dating applications have made us younger gays on edge, when in the past, there weren't as many distractions and, well, the Internet, when you dated before the dawn of the millennial gen-eration. I got a sense of hope because although there is a perversion of new sexual exploration, I find that most gay men I have interviewed or connected with prefer monogamy as a majority. Intimidation is huge for us gays. We have this inadequacy complex. Meaning, for monogamous men, the idea of opening a relationship sends a sharp jab to our ego. How to justify that on our behalf determines the thought process on experiencing an open relationship. It's about bal-ancing that to have a conversation in anything polyamorous. I have seen some people who have open relationships can walk the fine line to use their liaisons as coping mechanisms, which isn't good for any-one. We gay men should first establish some type of commitment rather than not committing to anything at all, and this works for both sides in some aspect: an appealing idea of trust.

The idea about open relationships that is the most frustrating to me is the "I have everything I want in this relationship, but I still want to see other people" mentality. That is like saying this ham-burger is perfect without the cheese and pickles. Then, my friends, that isn't the definition of *perfect*. This would be something that is sugarcoated as inadequate. If something is perfect, there is nothing that negates from the idea of the thing being referred as perfect. The end (takes a bow). This isn't a good fit for you, so you should adopt the "onward we go" mentality.

It angers me that we gay men already have so much stigma about being uncommitted and not being seen as being able to have a traditional partnership as the rest of society. So really, do we have to have this weird run-around about how we lead and view relation-ships? Can't we just do what everyone else does to sustain societal normalcy? Then again, some men would argue that this is what we are told to do, and that going with the grain isn't fair for their position on how they choose to love. For me, it seems like a good choice in going with the grain this time around. I just imagine the conversations at family get-togethers about introducing *both* these men as my partners. But, here is my monogamous nature trying to understand polyamory fully. We're already so overly sexualized in the media. If a partner resents you for not being sexually compatible, not having as much activity, etc., then you are in the wrong relationship from the get-go. From what I know of polyamorous men, those men are able to sanction a relationship. Meaning, they can give this piece of pie to someone who fulfills them emotionally and spiritually, but then they have to give another piece to someone else who allows them to explore their prevalent sexual tendencies and desires. These types of men aren't people I choose to work with, with sex being something that trumps a lot of other qualities they are looking for in a long-term partner. Emotional security trumps a huge portion of things that can bring a relationship into the red or green zone quite easily. I'm sorry, that gamble isn't something I care to even think about or even attempt to try. I remember telling a friend that it's almost like someone offering me meth. What does it say about me that you feel comfortable offering me something that I have a strong notion against? Meth is bad, and there is no way to convince me it will ever be good for someone. This is how I identify a general relationship and understand that my identity isn't everyone else's.

On the other hand, do friends with benefits really work? Um, yes, if both parties simply just want to get laid, and you communicate appropriately. I see this mostly happen during interludes of dating highs to lows in date practice. Boys will be boys. Heck, I've been there, done that. This process works with men in open relationships, but one has to be careful about attraction and chemistry development. This is something we cannot plan in advance for, in which this unexpected act can be very treacherous. Good news, though, we males are much better at that type of separation than our sensitive female counterparts. We can grab and go more easily. Males are very linear in their thought process, so once they have that specific animalistic urge, that's all they want at that moment. However, be very aware about the *moment after*. Is it always that simple? Most of the time, not really. The problem lies within the imbalance of expectation. Gay men experience this lifestyle in phases, no matter how I try to protect the idea of monogamy in our community. Being intimate with someone creates a bond and can cause an unexpected emotional response from one person, creating a type of internal imbalance. It's all about mind-set and permission in allowing yourself to be present in the formality of a standard relationship. The more serious you seem about a relationship, the more attractive you seem in a relationship, and the more you seem datable to most.

❦

A friend recently wrote this very eloquent article about what it means to be celibate. Her viewpoint came from a more religious implication, but I decided to take mine in a more realistic, more widely received point of view. The gay culture is pretty black-and-white when it comes to others labeling what defines infidelity. Usually there are some sorts of steps that lead up to these inclinations: drugs, alcohol, or simply a man wanting to be a playboy and not wanting to settle down. Yet there is still some sort of lie associated with this: saying that you want a long-term, monogamous relationship then wanting something else entirely.

Our culture is fairly open anyway. We're open to change, and a majority of the LGBT community would label themselves as socially liberal in comparison to our heterosexual counterparts. Therefore, a lot of our "rules" on how we view our own intimate relationships can seem looser. At the end of the day, we are sexual human beings, but if you are with someone you label as significant, and you catch him staring at the waiter, do you passively aggressively make a dig, or do you also chime in with the admiration? The same thing goes with pornography and sexual images in general. Do you become red with jealousy, or are you intrigued and create an open space to trust your partner in his discernment and separation?

Distinguish your own thought process between simple admiration and a habitual need. Are you just admiring the hunky swimsuit model on your own social media page, or do you find yourself searching for them multiple times a day? Sexual addiction is a real thing, just a disclaimer. Ask yourself, why do you need to look at porn or sexual imagery? Just to get off, something more surface and trivial, or is it for you to create a fantasy of feeling attractive or desired or to fill some type of void? Do you feel like you can only seek pleasure by creating a fantasy or with an actual human being whom you have been connecting with on an exclusive level? We should realistically call it as it is. Keep in mind, *cheating* means "to deceive," "to mislead," or "to act dishonestly." But if you have open communication with your partner, speak with truth and integrity, then you can't go wrong. If you feel it is wrong, be honest and verbal. Your partner will understand if he has a strong connection with you. I find that some gay men in long-term, committed relationships use pornography as a form of safe exploration to make their intimate lives more exciting. Yet when a couple starts opening their relationship in the actuality of physicality, I find that real emotions are being exchanged, and that's when I have seen relationships go down a very slippery slope fairly quickly, and usually with a feeling of betrayal and devastation.

∽⁂∾

I remember when I first came out as a gay man and was just petrified of any STD known to man. I remember giving a man a hand job, knowing he was HIV positive, and immediately thinking I had gotten it. I was doomed. Oh, and he probably had syphilis too. What's this mole on my back? I am dying tomorrow; I have cancer. I've heard people call this a stress spiral. We have all been there.

I began to target my fear. My fear came from the unknown. It was the unknown, meaning the lack of education I had on the virus and most other ones out there. The "knowledge is power" mantra rang so true to my soul at this point in my life.

I had dated a man with herpes for around three months, and it wasn't the end of the world. It was still a little tiptoey, though, and this is just coming from one of my insecurities. One of my best girlfriends, who now is in a very loving relationship with a husband and has a newborn at the moment, had it too. I remember just asking her plain and simple what it's like being in monogamous relationship and also having something that can potentially be caught by her partner. She just said it involved a lot of honesty and also her being responsible by being on medication.

I had an amazing opportunity to connect with a physician who had worked with the HIV positive community for almost eleven years. This medical professional had worked for a local prevalent healthcare foundation for an extended period of time, caring for mainly uninsured or underinsured individuals living with HIV. The majority of this physician's patients were mostly MSM (Men who have Sex with other Men) who had contracted the virus through unprotected sex, adding that we must not overlook the fact that HIV also affects the heterosexual and IV-drug-using populations.

I asked this medical professional about their experience, working with patients who are newly diagnosed with HIV. "There's been such amazing progress in antiretroviral therapies such that nowadays, I could look this person in the eye and assure him that with proper care and commitment to treatment, he could live a full and normal life expectancy. Despite this, however, I think being diagnosed with HIV is still an emotional experience for most. We've come a long way as a society, but there are still issues with stigma and discrimination. I think there is such an important prevention message in all of this. Yes, we can treat and control HIV, but it's still a lifelong disease without a cure... and it's preventable."

This segued nicely into the next topic we discussed: PrEP (Pre-Exposure Prophylaxis). When this medical professional left their practice, this person took a position with a very groundbreaking biopharmaceutical company that treats or very well prevents HIV infection. Doing my research, Truvada is only antiviral medication on the market that has been FDA approved for the prevention of HIV. "Condoms, when used correctly and consistently, can prevent HIV acquisition, but the reality for many is that condoms aren't used 100 percent of the time. For those individuals, Truvada can add an extra layer of protection. It needs to be taken daily to be effective, and it does require routine laboratory monitoring about every three months, so it's a decision that should be made after weighing your individual risks and benefits with your doctor." Just as a side note, PrEP doesn't protect you from everything else. I am trying to eradicate this stigma in our community that taking this one precaution doesn't make you immune to others.

I had a couple other medical professionals tell me that I don't really need it because of my lifestyle. I was recommended PeP (Post-Exposure Prophylaxis), which basically is only used as a precautious and emergent tool. It's one thing for me to be having sex with someone new every week, but the amount of sexual encounters I have had probably is below average to most gay men. I am also very responsible, get tested regularly (three to four times a year), and always use condoms. I can count the number of condomless sex I have had in my entire life on one hand, 90 percent of those experiences being with men I had been with for two-to-six-plus months.

In discussing HIV prevention, this physician also explained a concept to me that I found interesting: treatment as prevention. "The basic premise is that if someone is HIV positive and is well controlled on antiretroviral therapy [with an undetectable HIV viral load], his risk of transmitting HIV to a partner is exponentially lower than if he were not on treatment [with a high HIV viral load]. There have been mathematical models postulating that if we could identify every single person in a community who is HIV positive and put each and every one of them on treatment, the collective HIV viral load of that community would be undetectable, and we could essentially halt new infections. The unfortunate reality is that about 20 percent of people living with HIV are unaware of their infection, and these 20 percent are responsible for 50 percent of all new infections."

I also asked this medical professional about specific fluid exchange from sexual practices. She explained that, simply put, the virus is transmitted through infected blood and/or semen gaining access to an HIV negative individual's bloodstream. So for example, oral sex is low risk; for a transmission to occur, it would require the HIV positive partner to ejaculate *and* for that ejaculate to have access to the HIV negative partner's bloodstream via on open sore/cut in his mouth. By contrast, anal receptive sex is the highest risk, where the HIV positive partner's ejaculate could gain entry into the HIV negative partner's bloodstream through micro abrasions or tears in the anal mucosa.

We do shame so many of our gay brothers because of certain stigmas we have about men with HIV. Most of the relationships I've had with guys I had dated who were HIV positive didn't work because they were just assholes, or the chemistry fizzled, which is about their personality deficiency and not about their health status whatsoever. I have dated a couple that were actually very upfront about their status and were very respectful of me. It's your responsibility as a gay man to have those uneasy conversations from the beginning. I have seen accounts of many successful serodiscordant relationships (one HIV positive male and the other being HIV negative). They are mostly built on trust, communication, and preventative measures. The bottom line in all this is the importance of awareness. Be aware that sometimes people don't want to budge on their willingness to date someone with HIV. Our discriminatory-pointing fingers should be more transparent though, and we should have more open conversations rather than terse ones. Know your risk, protect yourself, and get tested regularly. Never be afraid to have an adult conversation before you mess around with anyone. Don't be a fool; wrap your tool, gents.

A Cop and a Robber

I remember sitting at a local leather bar, with a couple of good friends during San Diego Pride. Not my cup of tea, but whatever. Happy Pride. Conversations of bathhouses were in my ear, and it seemed exciting because I had never been to one. I find that culture fascinating. Maybe I find it intriguing because it's something that is very exposed, but I don't think I could do it. I never went, but I remember thinking how much I had grown up as a gay man. Instead of being terrified over the idea, I just realized that it just wasn't for me. I was definitely the pink elephant in the room, in the dim lightning with torture-ish devices adorning the walls. I remember thinking, *When in Rome...* It's hard to make me feel out of place a lot of times. I'm mostly accepting of everyone as they are, whether society labels it abnormal or not.

I met this man on another popular dating application, really not expecting too much. He spends a week out of a month in San Diego and then the rest in LA. He was really close and was charming, so he met up with my friends and me for a quick drink. These friends were the best friends of my ex. I loved how we were explaining what "the divorce" meant within our friendship. They both actually met on another dating application: "The [insert dating app name here] date that never went away," as he so eloquently labeled. They are now happily married, and I am ecstatic for them. Anyway, I liked the idea of meeting someone new and hearing their story. I definitely felt instantaneous protection and chemistry from this man, especially as soon as this man grazed my thigh when he was complimenting me. He worked in law enforcement. I was no stranger to that lifestyle, most of my paternal extended family being in that field. I was completely sober, but he enticed me with his hot tub, and I obliged. I was intrigued by him.

We walked to his North Park place, an up-and-coming funky fresh part of San Diego. I remember feeling safe. When we got to his place, I liked that it was pretty ordinary. We sat and talked on his couch, and that's when we started making out and eventually made our way back to his bedroom. We did mostly third-base-type stuff. I did tell him that I eventually wanted that hot tub experience he originally baited me with.

We woke up the next morning, and he had a couple of phone calls he warned me about. One of which he was on for an entire hour while I was waking up next to him. I felt it was weird that he was trying to be touchy-feely with me while "working." After that, I had to go back to the place where I was staying and gather some things. He had another Skype call with his life coach when we returned, which lasted another hour and a half. He didn't expect me, so he had work to do. I understood. I didn't seem to mind. However, I remember looking up at the ceiling, alone on his bed, and I knew right then and there that something was off. This man was in a balancing act: kind of like the circus performer on a flat board, which is on a moving ball, with boxes of different weights in his hands. I remember telling him, "Do you always work on Sundays?" We then walked to a nearby restaurant, and we got to know each other a little more. I could tell this man had an amazing heart, but there was something blocking him. As I am getting older, I am getting much keener in noticing this in gay men and right away. Darn it, it's a gift I love and hate. I find that men I date tell me I am predicting too much, but I'm usually correct. I'll tell you when I'm wrong, I promise. I'm not afraid of that, but trust me. I wouldn't say that I make quick judgments; I've met many men both professionally and personally that have a certain air about them when I know their life has equilibrium. We as perceptive humans can sense that too, even in something as simple as the Starbuck's line.

We spent the rest of Pride skipping around like giddy high school lovers, me meeting a couple of his friends. I remember sitting at a bar and getting to know his attractive middle-aged friend who loved boyish white surfer dudes, while he stood next to me and talked to this one guy for what seemed to be a half hour. I thought nothing of it at that time, but this will make sense soon. I was worried about getting to LA at an appropriate time and being sober for that trek. He sent a car for me back to the place I was staying, and off I went into the sunset.

Weeks passed by, and I really started seeing the escalation of the communication block. He didn't want to do real sex and would say, "Sex is going to be so good with you." Another block. In his line of work, he was consistently busy and not near his phone. So sometimes it would be five or more hours before I would get a response from him; after, he would ask me a direct question. Maybe I was making a mountain out of a molehill, but maybe this was when I started seeing a pattern that made me uncomfortable.

We had planned for me to come see him after one of my work's speed dating events since it was close to where he lived. You know, a "Netflix and chill" situation. Easy. I am usually exhausted after event days, and preplanning this was amazing and perfect in my book. I remember after my event, I had picked us up some pizza for dinner and texted him to let him know I was on my way to his place. As I was passing the hustle and bustle of the West Hollywood gay scene, I got a text telling me to meet him at a popular Mexican bar in the gayborhood. I was perturbed at this idea, because all my friends knew that me going out on a Tuesday means that hell might have frozen over by a polar vortex. Nonetheless, after a very long workday, I parked, walked over, and sure enough, there he was, multiple drinks in, with his charming, affluent older friend from out of town. I liked that with his friend, you couldn't tell that he was a lot richer than he let out. His friend had many great stories, and as always, the conversation turned into what types of men he liked. If I remember correctly, he loved boyish Asian men since he had spent some time in Asia. I would say a half hour passed by, and my date was talking to some guy at the bar. His friend was even saying, "Maybe I should get our drinks myself." He came back, with a snide smile, and I, already being somewhat angry, smiled and was cordial. He said something about how the guy he was talking to was against cops, and that struck a very intense conversation, in a bar. Strike. I honestly don't remember what I said to him on my way back to his place. Knowing myself, not much. I didn't want to be seen as a crazy person with all these unrealistic expectations. I went back to his place, placed the now cold pizza in the fridge. I think we fooled around then went to bed. Whenever I start to say, "I think we fooled around," that's when I know things are on a downward spiral. Make every moment extraordinary and memorable if you feel a person is listening to you. I always give a person the benefit of the doubt, but sometimes, that's a fault I have. Maybe call it me being oblivious. Maybe I should take my own advice.

I had planned another night with him. I had a game night with some friends in the Valley and was having a great time. Most of them were actors, which can be quite entertaining. I had gotten to the party early, and there was just three of us having "girl" time. I had voiced to them that the current guy I was seeing wasn't picking up on cues that weren't kosher with me. I needed to feel like he was excited about seeing me. To my dismay, I left my friends and made the late trek up the 405 to see him. For those of you who don't know, doing this act is a sight and an act of God indeed. I thought it would be cute for him to take the Five Love Languages® test when I arrived, as I was getting ready for bed. Then after being in his bed alone for a little while, he returned back to me with a computer in his hand, updating his website for work. He did this for what seemed to be an hour or two. I remember watching a movie and looking up at him, hoping he would put his work away and acknowledge my presence. In my peripheral vision, I noticed a name I recognized. Turns out, this guy was someone I had interviewed to be matched with my clients, and he disclosed to me how they were in a relationship for a long time and still worked together professionally. I was frustrated, because I was trying to ask him about their relationship while I was lying next to him, and he seemed distracted. I wasn't trying to pry, I was simply perplexed knowing both of them so well at that point. It was more like, "How the hell did that work." The guy he had dated was a very pretty guy who was known to prefer dating African American pro football players. I have to admit, the next day, I did a little social media stalking, and there they were together in old photos. I still remember having to pick my lower jaw off the floor while at my desk. They were polar opposites. In their case, in my opinion, opposites didn't attract, and I got that it seemed tumultuous for a while. I felt bad that what seemed to be such a kind man subjected himself to a person that didn't inspire him to be a better him.

I am only human and can sometimes not be the best communicator, but I remember passive-aggressive exchanges between us that finally led to a phone call about how this man didn't see what he was doing was wrong. I remember repeating to him, "You are not getting it. You are not getting me." This conversation was going on an endless circle. He was seeing me as not being understanding, probably close to selfish or overbearing. He said that he had work to do, that his friend surprised him from out of town, blah, blah. He wouldn't call me or would plan to and not do it, when I was trying to explain to him that my feelings where hurt and that they had festered. He wasn't seeing that the issue wasn't from the choice, but from how the choice was done. *Dude, just tell me you want to work or cancel our plans ahead of time like an adult* is what I remember thinking. Yeah, I still might be disappointed, but maybe you'll make it up to me, and at least you are being mature and honest. He assumed that I would have been so easygoing with everything, which I am, but not if I start feeling disposable or my feelings feel unimportant. Later I told him, "When you realize that what you did to me was not nice, that's when I can start talking to you again."

Weeks passed by, and my birthday rolled around, and we had another passive-aggressive moment, and I basically told him that we were adults and we should throw the pride out the window. The coffee date he promised me never happened.

Fast-forward three months, and his name crossed my mind. I knew he had a recent surgery, so I thought to check in on him. He seemed different. He told me that he still had a sexy picture of me in his bed from San Diego. I always stay classy; let's learn from celebrities in the tabloids to never take nudes. *Ever.* He was very descriptive and sexual and told me he had recently thought of me as well. He was being communicative and, also for the first time, was honest about his feelings and genuinely apologized. I told him we both deserved happiness and balance in our lives. I also told him this was the first time he had talked to me *like this*. After some of his cute sexting (mind you, I used to be completely turned off by this, but now I am all right with it), I was somewhat turned on, to be candid, and before I knew it, I said we should chat more in person that evening. I knew something or someone had changed him overtime. I packed a bag, with my cold breakfast oatmeal in hand, and made my journey west from my eastern abode.

I entered his place, gave him a quick peck on the lips, and then we made our way back to his bedroom. With a sadistic and gory horror movie playing in the background, we were catching up with each other. I frankly asked him, "Why am I here?" I honestly don't remember what he said back, which foreshadowed some future events between us. He started massaging my hands then my legs. He kept looking at the movie, then me, then the movie, and finally I said, "Well, are you going to kiss me?" After some passionate kissing that I had forgotten, his smooth hands started to rub right above my zipper.

I remember us really embracing each other, and as we were about to do the deed, I said, "You still owe me dinner. I want this to last." Side note, I also tried poppers for the first time that night, and you are not missing much. Just take a whiff of a permanent marker, hooray. It was so strange to me to do something in which he wanted to hold off on in our couple of months together. He told me he "wanted something deeper." Gosh, what am I doing to elicit this response in the men I date? Do I scream "slut that doesn't have any weight to him"? After we washed up, we had briefly talked about the guys we were dating. For me, I was still trying to get first dates, but he told me he was "dating but taking things slow." I lay next to him, thinking that I was now staring at a changed man. I knew something or someone had changed him. He turned to me and later said, "You are extremely intuitive." I had visited two or three psychics in my life, and they confirmed that I had some psychic abilities, whatever that means. I sensed a bit of confusion and sadness in his eyes. "I'm confused. This will be the last time I will have sex with another person." Pause. It's like the room froze, gravity collapsed, and I told him, "You love *him*." I honestly felt my exchange with him was cinematic. Was I the sexual mistress on the side that had only pure intentions but now felt used? Through jumbled words, the "slow" relationship he was referring to happened to be going on for four or five months now. They were seeing each other twice a week. Maybe even when we were even dating. I try not to think about the timelines and how they might have intersected. This didn't seem slow to me at all. Turns out this was the guy, I assume, that changed his mind-set on things. Yes, on paper, the exclusive conversation didn't happen, but because of the time we spent together, the conversations of growth we explored, and then the straight-up deceit that I felt—it was differing territory to me. What an asshole. Please do yourself a favor and be honest with men you date when things become physically intimate on a continuous basis. No one wants some stranger's tainted cooties. Deep breath. He said, "I need to tell him to not see anyone else anymore." I told him, "You should tell him eventually what happened. He deserves that. I don't think the 'I needed to have sex with someone else to realize how much I love you' talk is a good idea, but in time. He shouldn't know who I am, but he needs to know. That's fair. You wouldn't want him to do the same thing to you." I asked him how they met and discovered that he was slightly younger than me, hunky, and going to graduate school. At the end of the day, I am no match for love. I could have been angry with him for using me as some testing pawn, but I thought to myself, *There is no point.* I remember telling him, "There's a change in energy about you." He concluded, "I'm learning to communicate more." I asked, "Where did you learn that?" I giggled, but that was the moment that I realized that this man was ready to love. "I feel like I am finally ready," he said. I told him about how I saw the same energy in guys who interview with me to be matched, called "the switch". This is when I know a man is truly ready and can feel it in his heart, mind, soul, and body that he is ready to accept and share the true essence of love with another human being. I lay there in the deepest part of my vulnerability, basically naked, and I felt thankful for him despite his treating me like partially chewed gum under his shoe. I felt stillness and a sense of calm. I told him that what he did to me didn't make it right, but what I told him was that I was happy for him. I also told him that I would still be his friend and that I wouldn't leave him in that sense, but that any future romantic progression would end. "I can't be placed in this position again," I remember saying.

I was still indifferent and saddened that Thursday. I kept running the "How do people do these things to other people? I'm a good person." My workday seemed invalid. My headspace felt vacant. I felt like everyone around me was Charlie Brown's teacher in slow motion. I know he had said that he wanted to remain friends, so the next morning, I requested his friendship on Facebook. We had a lot of the same mutual friends, naturally, so sometimes I stumble on his feed. Turns out, he had accessed his account that day, but didn't accept me. Then it hit me like a violent wave. This man has lied to me yet again. He wasn't going to be my friend. This was just another ploy that I fell for, again. I was nice to him three times: before, during, and after everything. I felt like he stabbed me in the back and watched me bleed with a smirk on his face and then left me alone. What really drove the knife in my back was the fact that he and his *other* were now meeting his friends later that same night and watching the show *Scandal* together. Literally, I spent the wee hours of the morning with this man, and now he was with his other that night, and with his friends.

Never in my life have I been intentionally snarky, but I wrote him one last message: "Enjoy *Scandal*. Seems fitting. Please delete my number." Sometimes I wonder if me coming forward about his true character during his election in a public office would have made a great show. Lucky for him, I am not a vengeful person.

In the early hours of that Thursday morning, with my overnight bag and cold oatmeal, I felt a sense of hopelessness, and I packed a sense of guilt and pride in the same black canvas. Turns out that was the moment I knew that I needed to share my voice in a public medium. Turns out that I was the one serving and protecting, but another man stole my heart like a bandit. Thank you to the man who made me feel safe for a moment: you are the reason for the start of this journey and my book.

Divorcing Your Job for Love

"I am a married man, and I have worked for my love and keep working for it. It has made me understand that love is not something that comes naturally. You have a natural attraction to the other person, yes. Flowers are natural, but earth has to work to water them. The key word is all of this is *work*. You show up to your job because you want to. Nobody is making you go. It's the same with love. You work at it, and something beautiful can result. Look, if you are a busy person, say, 'I am a busy person, I can't text you too much.'" This short testimony was impactful to me and hopefully you too.

I am a sucker for making the best first impression possible. I remember meeting this one guy online one summer, and we were casually messaging back and forth. Funny thing, he actually recognized me from my line of work. He would sometimes wait days and maybe even a week to respond to my messages. He was super wishy-washy about meeting too, it seemed. Geeze, dude, I already tried to schedule something with you. Now it's your turn. I thought he was plainly too busy, or I wasn't his cup of tea fully, so I kept it really casual and tried not to give it too much expectation. I had told him I had met someone, and I paused our intermittent chatting. Three months later, I had broken up with the same guy, and we started chatting again after the hustle and bustle of the holidays started to dissipate. He finally asked if he could give me a call, and I was filled with excitement. Hours later, he then texted me his schedule. I was a bit perplexed because I was thinking, *Is he really scheduling a call with me?* I had never had that happen before. I mean, just pick up the damn phone, and if I don't answer, there's this little thing called a voice mail. He told me, "I was going to ask what day worked for you but instead gave you my schedule since it's all over the place, sorry about that. Let me know whatever day works for you ... it's

just so that we are both on the same page as to when we are free."
I was really honest and basically said maybe we should just wait to
reschedule when things are a bit lighter with his workload. I felt this
was an agenda already, and he was so quick to tell me he was so "easy
going." It just seemed so odd to talk to someone after "11:00 p.m.
the next day, or 6:00 p.m. the following" when this was the first time
I would be solidifying an impression of him. He told me I was possibly judging him too harshly, but if I compiled everything collectively
in the many months we had chatted, he seemed like he didn't have
balance at all. After all, he did say that his "schedule was all over the
place." When the time came for our call, I had texted him right at
the scheduled time, and he texted three minutes later, saying that he
"was working until 11:30 p.m. that night and off early tomorrow at
6:30 p.m. Unless [I wanted to chat] later on tonight" with a smiley
face emoticon at the end. Mind you, there were three days of silence
between the initial booking and his response. WTF. I hope you are
a doctor, number 1. And number 2, no, I don't want to talk to you.
Congrats, you just blew it. Needless to say, I didn't respond because I
felt the universe didn't want us to meet. With most of the men I had
dated in the past, it was so easy for us to call and initially meet. That's
why a lot of dating applications give you a time limit of a week or two
to meet before they disappear—they are teaching us a thing called
accountability and responsibility. This was not in our cards, and I
stepped away with a smile on my face. Everything seemed staggered
and not naturally fluid. He didn't realize that his behavior screamed
he was a workaholic and not being a respectful dater. He could have
easily texted me on his lunch, since obviously a huge majority of
people know where and when they are working a day or more in
advance. I was at that point in my life where I wanted my partner
to put me before his career, because I would do the same. Emotional
success trumps financial success: most successful relationships have
that ideal.

I am noticing a huge trend that could be seen as a tool of awareness for a lot of entrepreneurial people. One very normal trait my
clientele requests in my interview process is an ambitious and hard-
working man, a man who is financially stable, which normally has a

positive domino effect on a person's emotional and physical stability. I get it; most of us gay men are transplants in Los Angeles (or any other major metropolitan city) in some way, and want to make ourselves and the significant others around us proud. We feel that we have to fight tooth and nail to get where we want to or feel like we are right there with everyone else. In this process, we are willing to sacrifice anything and everything to get to that crystal clear goal, our diamond in the rough. One theory I have is that we gay men feel like we have gone through an additional life process of coming out that a lot of "the other" working professionals haven't experienced. Sometimes this gives us a sense of entitlement or pragmatism.

I have gotten to know a lot of men from my daily conversations that are in their early thirties or higher and have never had a long-term relationship. A lot of times they have had a few that lasted three months at most. Trust me, I am no judge. I am just seeing this in the eyes of the person I set you up with. How attractive does that sound to your dater? It makes you sound like a guy who is afraid of commitment, or you just don't have any relationship education or that you never have time to date. I call it being relationship retarded, not to be politically incorrect. There is nothing I can do as your matchmaker, but present facts to your dater about you. Obviously, I'm packaging you to be as attractive to your dater as possible, and I never go into a relationship résumé. It'll come out soon enough, though, if you are dating someone smart. The opinions are made by the other person, and remember, first impressions are everything.

Divorce your job and only allow yourself visitation rights is my simple mantra. Meaning, see your job as conditional rather than an impermeable shield that nothing can go through. Think logically for a second. If you want children and you are just starting to date at the peak of your career, it will probably take you at least a couple more years to gain some insight on what you don't and do want in your ideal mate. Gay men can sometimes have that pressure by the sociographic factors throughout their upbringing. Dating is a long, growing process, keep in mind. You fall down to make the getting up easier. Don't get me wrong; I've seen gay men in their forties make great first parents. However, they can agree that it's just a little harder when you are simply older. No one ain't getting younger, and most people feel they don't look as hot as they did in their younger years. The good news is that, in my experience, most gay men aren't set on children. If I met ten men, one or two might really want kids. The majority of the rest want kids only if their partner was excited about having them too. I also find that most men are okay with men with kids already, but usually only if they are independent, and there's a huge balance there. No one wants to feel like they aren't as important. I am in the selfish boat here. I want to travel, see the world, build a home, and babies are expensive and time-consuming. Thank God my brother took the grandparent baton from me. Make a difference somehow in others, yourself, and the world; clock out, and leave it behind the door. No one wants to hear how busy you are. Everyone is busy all the time, no matter if your career is in Los Angeles, especially. No one goes around saying how much ample free time they have while skipping freely through a prairie of daffodils, because everyone clearly has time to just do that.

Looking over the years, I would always like the idea of dating men in their early forties and would always come up empty-handed. It always seems like a certain presumed fallacy where I felt, well, if they are older, they ought to know what they want and have their shit together by now. I find that a lot of successful and entrepreneurial gay men lack work and personal life balance. Not everyone, but maybe I can speak for most hustle-and-bustle cities and the characteristics of the gay men that reside in them. I remember getting so frustrated about men who automatically wanted me to understand that their meeting was running late, their day got a lot busier, or they had to cancel our date because of this deadline. This might have been the second or third time this has happened. Eye roll. Shit happens, I get it. A pattern is a choice. Did this person realize that I cancelled a dinner date with a close friend, went to the office early to be able to leave early, just for the tentative option to spend an hour with a stranger, while patiently waiting an hour of traffic to go eight miles for a cocktail? I'll say, if I were in love with someone, this person would be a priority. I want a guy to say, "I'm sorry I only have ten minutes. I have a date tonight, and I don't want to be late.

Should we reschedule?" That makes you look like you offer good balance both in and out of the boardroom. If you prioritize your love life over your professional one, chances are it will have more opportunity to flourish. As a reminder, no plant grows on its own. What does a rich life mean to you? Is it more about fiscal success or a life full of fond memories and having a good conversation over Chinese takeout? If you flake more than once on someone, don't expect a response back, and if you do, you better owe this person big time. If you feel you don't owe anyone anything, you should have your mother turn you over her knee and whip the self-righteous ego out of you. You could easily say, "You are being way too serious too quickly." This is about respect and being practical. I am just as capable of balancing my meetings to keep my commitment just as much as anyone else. Needless to say, I am excellent with my time, and that expectation reflects my ability to date responsibly and ethically. I don't have time to deal with constant excuses, although emergent situations happen. No man deserves to feel like you are impeding his day, ever. No one should feel like they're only important when they are only convenient for you. Let the person know that they are valued and that making time for them is important. Are you too old to be playing games? Probably, if you are reading this book with a third eye.

On the other side, a really close friend of mine went through a dark period in her life where work was a numbing mechanism for her. She worked fourteen-plus hours a day just to cover up on some personal issues she was dealing with. Instead of relying on people who cared deeply for her, she relied on making as much money as fast as she possibly could. Yes, she was financially happy, but would tell me she felt unfulfilled. Her body was craving courtship, deep relationships, and you could see the neon sign above her flashing for it. The "I'll sleep when I'm dead" mentality probably rang true for her at that time, but it seemed she felt dead when she was alive and breathing. She has now found her Price Charming, and he definitely keeps her in check.

Something one past boyfriend did that irked me at times was getting in these consistent huffy moods because work had been so stressful on a very regular basis. I wanted him to leave it at the door so we could just enjoy each other. His mother said that he was such a caring, generous, and loving person growing up. He was a passionate guy; it was in his DNA. In some jobs growing up, I felt like I was overqualified and not appreciated, and I would sometimes voice that. We're both human, right? We both can feel overworked and undervalued. "It never ends," he sometimes would say. At the end of the day, yes, it can end. I now choose to work hard from my desk for eight hours maximum, three to five times a week, and then I turn it off. Do not ask me to get back to you on a weekend regarding work. It can wait until Monday, I promise. I take offense at times because I saw him taking the stress of his job with him, everywhere, via conversations with friends and social media. Sometimes this topic leeched into our relationship naturally. I always say that the more you talk about something, the more power you give the emotion behind it. When someone asks me about my day, I usually am very brief about it, even though the whole world melted down and I somehow had to glue it back together with my teeth. There's a difference between something that's normative and a friend you haven't seen in a while who is genuinely inquisitive about your general well-being. The more I talk about the frustrations of the day, the more I get into it again. I am a matchmaker, so most of my days are filled with saving people from the depths of dating despair. I am fanning fires, and I am putting them out with hopefully no damage. No use in wasting that energy, in my opinion. But then again, you shouldn't bottle things up. That is why my personal fitness regimen allows me to create that release, and you should find yours.

I remember working with this one client who was fairly young, successful, and handsome. He was a great dater and made great first impressions. How would a guy like him need a matchmaker? Well, a lot of our clients hire a matchmaker to be able to deal with schedules and weed through the crazies and time wasters. All they want is to just show up and enjoy themselves. The thing about him was that he always abroad, across the country, only in town for a week in one month. His issue was that he was a feather in the wind. He would then get depressed, complaining how dating was difficult, and my initial response was that he had no weight for men looking for someone who wishes to settle down, in any capacity.

A lot of us entrepreneurial men suffer from something called time poverty. We are all so apt at planning our days way in advance for others, with little to no reward for us to be able create pauses in our day for selfish reasons. It almost correlates with a very heavy workout regimen. We must rest to make our muscles grow and to build strength over time. Same goes with relationships. It's so easy for me to label someone who consistently tells me his workdays are packed and he has a big travel schedule coming up as too busy. I have already thrown in the towel. Tell him what you can do, not can't. Optimism will trump pessimism every time. I just want you to show up, that's all; I don't care to hear about the prowess of your ambitious nature. Usually, that will emerge naturally. I finally feel that I have somewhat of a good balance now, but my friends are trained to ask for my time ahead of time. Most of my friends follow the same model, so it actually works out to both our advantages. The thing, though, is that we ask. If you live a lifestyle of regimens, know that spontaneity will never work in the beginning when getting to know someone. It's the way the cookie crumbles, and those spurts of unplanned things will come in time when both parties have found their groove, and the attraction grows.

I am all about the hustle, though. You know, doing what you have to do to make your dreams come true. We gay men have this insatiable and intrepid nature that gives us yearning for dominance in a certain way. I remember having those jobs where I accepted the precedence that I was there specifically to earn a paycheck. I felt uninspired on a daily basis. I accepted these filler jobs just as that, so I do understand the adamant nature of earning a dime to pay your rent. We've all been there, and most of the time not by choice. As we grow up and become wiser, sometimes we do have a choice. I had a mentor once tell me that if you are working more than forty hours a week, you are not allocating your time efficiently. I remember a friend mentioning to me that the editor of a very popular fashion publication only allows seven-minute meetings, or something specific like that, so there you go. I firmly believe that if you work incessantly constantly, you are undervaluing yourself and your work ethic, and other people are letting you do it. Saying no has a profound power of meaning of professionalism.

I really try to make every moment I have with my significant other be positive, empowering, and easy. *Busy* people have many goals and complain they have no time, but *productive* people set priorities and let their results speak for themselves. The ones whom are the quietest usually make the most noise in this sense. Life is way too short to work through it all. Balance is pivotal; utilize it, and I promise you won't regret it.

Label Maker

Nowadays we as a society put so many labels on other individuals instantaneously. I myself can be guilty of this, but if I do, it's mostly based on recurring behavioral patterns from a scientific point of view. It's almost like we want to make sense of people without giving them a chance to defend themselves or to prove us wrong based on a stigma or societal inclination. When I go home to Georgia, people stare at me because I am wearing a leather jacket, a fedora, and my favorite pair of fitted semidesigner jeans. Trust me, being in LA is just depressing. I feel like a solid 7 there, and then everywhere else in the country view me as a runway model (or maybe that is what I would like for them to think). I guess that explains the judgmental glares when I only want some organic produce from the local Georgian supermarket and call it a day. Gay men especially blindly assume which type of fruits should be matched with certain physical stature. I don't like to be assumed as a twink who must be a power bottom. I ran into this assumption when I dated men over forty especially. They never really saw me as their equal, but viewed themselves as someone who was older, wiser, and presumably needed to take the lead. I'm sorry, I'm fine. I can march to the own beat of my own drum, thank you. Men under thirty, I found, that even though their physical type didn't matter, I was mostly drawn to their internal, which was not as successful and mature as I would have hoped. Most men who are a lot like me have somewhat of the same viewpoint. Because we are such a physical and eye-driven species, we like to immediately categorize and compartmentalize men based on what we think we know of them. This comes from our desire as humans to make sense of things, and this was even installed in us from our childhood. I think this type of thinking attributes to things like racism and feminism. We were always taught that a certain color block goes on top of this one, and that this wooden log fits on this one to make a finished structural product. Patterns make sense to us. This normally is guided heavily by social stigma too as opposed to individualized, intimate interaction.

We sometimes only want to see past the thrill of a "point A to point B surface-based" concept and then move on to someone else. Um, yes, that's easier, but it doesn't make sense if you wish to date long-term. If you feel like your tally of one-night stands outnumber your long-term relationships significantly, you might need a wrench for your well-oiled machine, no pun intended. A lot of those stigmas are reasonable assumptions based on the characteristics of our community in general. Every part of our visual capacity is being attacked at all angles, multiple times a day. Everywhere you look, your feed on any social media outlet are dudes with their shirts off. As you drive down the road, you see chiseled-bodied men in underwear ads, and even when you do go out for a drink, you are surrounded by infamously adorned Adonis-bodied go-go dancers. The thing that gets me the most in our community is the perversion of being physically stimulating in an immediate sense. I mean, look at dating applications nowadays. You only have a few seconds to prove yourself, with a single click or a swipe. It's a "hot or not" mentality. As a gay community, we must start learning to discern through physicality and allow the permeation of personality traits to be able to sway our sexual desires or assumptions. Someone's hotness is not an indication of their goals or personality. This societal comparison can infiltrate a person's confidence and self-esteem. They feel as if keeping up with the Joneses is an impossible feat. Emotional stability carries relationship longevity. Keeping this anchored in my mind helps me not judge others so blindly. I remember trying to date really openly in my first few years as a gay man. Although my search is more refined nowadays, I stopped any preconceived notions and sometimes just dated someone who was easy to converse with and showed up on time on our date. That was already a step above.

Notice when you do see a twink dating a daddy, as a gay society, we automatically think *escort*. Or how we can label a perfect jock dating a bigger bear as an oxymoron. Although, I do advocate that similar life experience plays into relationship longevity, age differences and physical type can be just what they are at times. I dated a guy once for around six months who was not physically active at all, very tall and lanky, tattooed, hipstery, who was more into very indie music and whiskey. He wasn't my physical type at all, but it just worked somehow. Sometimes taking a leap has its advantages. Sometimes I have those older men try to convince me that at twenty-five, the guy he's been seeing is "mature for his age." I'm sorry, if he's under twenty-eight and you are over forty, I find that leap of faith to be the biggest one of their lifetime. I normally do not interview anyone under twenty-five anyway. There is always an exception to the rule.

Ageism is something I have gotten flack for over the years in regard to this observation. I am all about love, in all its facets. When doing some research, a study of 3,000 individuals gave me the solid number of success rates in regard to age differences. A five-year age gap statistically means you're 18 percent more likely to divorce, that rate rises to 39 percent for a 10-year age difference, and 95 percent for a 20-year age gap. I think it doesn't matter what type of these relationships are, as I am assuming a plethora was taken for us to correlate something from this control group. If a connection works, it works, regardless of age. I'm not one to judge. The "love is love" mantra is quite endearing, but we have to pay close attention to the authenticity of that match. Is there a hidden agenda for either party? In my career, I've probably been able to successfully match 5 men together who are over 15 years or more apart. Most of those men where also both older than 35, from what I recall. I do see a stark difference between homosexual and heterosexual relationships, and how that is viewed differently in society, in regard to age difference. I pay little attention to those societal pressures or norms. In this instance, I verified, in person, that these two gay men seem to have similar lifestyles and points in their lives. This is 5 out of 100's, if I were to go into a more definitive quantifying statement. There's always a minority that I see, a rarity, but I collect more from the majority. So, there's a correlation I can draw from that, based on a business regarding matchmaking. I have to be pragmatic in this way, to offer a certain result to achieve something attainable in value. This isn't a thing about me being discriminatory or homophobic, but this is me being able to offer a success rate based on my experience of matching someone successfully, however the client defines that. I am only acting in the best interest of my client, and that is something a client requests in his search, and not something I oppress or sway on him. It honestly depends on the person; sometimes unintentional flukes happen in connection. Being unique is so much more fun to match than the gay normal. A lot of men in our community are not hot bodied, tan, and gorgeous. Those types of men have their own set of issues. They walk a fine line being looked at as a sex object, an idol, rather than an actual human being. The most interesting men I have been with are quite normal in every way. I find myself asking men I interview, what makes them weird? People are intrigued by being unique. From my standpoint, I notice that like-minded men attract each other more in the physical realm. We're just physical beings in our anatomical makeup. A much more stout man wanting to date a nineteen-year-old Asian boy, however, is probably for some sort of specific sexual pleasure, and that is a whole 'nother ball game.

⊷❧

If someone asked you, "How gay are you?" how would you respond? As a gay man myself, I find myself judging myself a lot. I find that we gay men sometimes actively shame ourselves in our masculinity whether we are out of the closet or not. A friend of mine referred me to a face tatted hairstylist that was closer to where I was residing one day. This barbershop was a little more street than my hairstylist in the Valley, who would talk about his long-distance relationship with his hot young Chilean boyfriend. I find myself thinking about how I spoke and saying the word *dude* or *man*. What am I, in high school again?

I would like to think that I have a good balance of both masculine and feminine traits. Scientific studies have heavily suggested that a male becomes homosexual based on certain hormone absorption in the fetus from a woman during her pregnancy. Also, gay men can have a larger corpus callosum, the central portion of the brain that separates it and facilitates interhemispheric communication. We're born this way, folks. I was chatting with a gay friend of mine, and he brought up the Kinsey Scale. Established in 1947, The Kinsey Institute describes this 0 to 6 scale as "a percentage reported exclusively (of) homosexual behavior and attractions, (and how) many individuals disclosed behaviors or thoughts somewhere in between."

People ask me all the time about my theory of opposites attracting, and my answer is yes and no. Sometimes logistic similarities can be awesome, like a work schedule. There is always an imbalance in this particular scale with gay men specifically. One guy is always a number higher or lower than the other; the numbers together could balance each other out somehow. The synergy of the relationship seems balanced because strengths and weaknesses are easily distributed in regard to the relationship as a whole. Sometimes it's only a fraction, but there is usually a difference. In one of my past relationships, I dated a man who was super hygienic, having an eight-step process in his shower ritual, whereas I am not that finicky. He can cook frozen fish and vegetables only, whereas I am super domestic, doing laundry, hosting parties, cleaning, and cooking much better meals. We had a certain balance. Do a quick inventory of your past long-term relationships. I just did. I was always the more masculine or the more feminine one. By no means is this a defamation of character and pride, but purely factual.

The scale also suggests that it can differ over time. Meaning, one month I could be more or less than the previous. This depends on the (non) progression of my relationship status or conditional factors like environment, i.e., being a regular at a nightclub with go-go dancers one month versus being a regular at swanky lounges in other months following. I have seen studies of twins that one day, they switch over favoring their mother and father. This seems to be a good parallel to create a notion of a natural "switch" over time.

Based on this scale, our culture can usually associate a bigger guy to be more masculine, a 0 to 3, and a leaner build to be more effeminate, a 3 to 6. Although, I have seen very muscular men be the more effeminate one, but they'll usually date a more masculine version of themselves. So as you can see, sometimes your physical being is just a shell that serves as a conduit to the internal thought process of someone.

I know hearing about people's various encounters on dating applications specifically really draws attention to the issue of masculinity. I know I have been reading a lot about it in the media as of late. I see a lot of verbiage like "masc only. masc4masc. masc?" I'm sure you see it too.

Coming from our business perspective, it's a definite preference, I have come to find. But because of mainstream dating application practices, it really convolutes that idealism and makes it almost discriminatory, e.g., "He isn't masculine enough." I would say I've met masculine guys who say they want to meet other guys like him because normally they like the same recreational things, like camping, cars, sports, and dive bars. I once had a fairly effeminate client that would rather date a guy like him, not outdoorsy, a fashionista, no facial hair, who fancies long five-course dinners. I am also speaking from a majority; there are those people who mix well. It's all relative. Sometimes, simplicity is just feeling it in the law of attraction in its nominal form.

I really got to thinking why we have "masculine only" as a stark preference. My theory is that a lot of it has to deal with sexual chemistry and perceived position preference. Let me tell you now, I have met many masculine guys that have disclosed to me that they are mostly bottoms and effeminate ones be tops. I saw one thing on a dating application once saying something along the lines of, "Just because you are all about muscle, that doesn't mean a purse can fall out of your mouth." The "looks can be deceiving" mantra rings true here, through this observation. Of course, I never utilize this preference when I am matching because I match mostly on energy, personality traits, commonalities, and life timeline. "Diva-esk" men seem like partiers and uncommitted to most other gay men. Which, looking from the outside in, makes them appear that they are not ready for something long-term. Of course, I've met many men like that who are quite the opposite, but remember, we are quite the surface culture.

I then look at my personal dating résumé, and most of the men I have dated in my past were on the masculine side. For me, it had to do with commonalities in our personalities. For instance, I have no desire to be caught up in pop culture references, and I don't have too strong opinions about people or most things. Also, men with flamboyant, overly gregarious, or ostentatious personalities tend to overwhelm me quite easily. My energy preference is more on the placid side. Regardless, date with an open eye rather than a squinted one.

I had casually polled a couple of gay men and asked their opinions on this topic. Some were from a societal point of view, some more political:

> Part of the reason of being gay is due to an attraction to masculine qualities in men. I will say "masculinity" is hardly ever perceived as a negative trait, deeply rooted in how humanity in general has functioned for ages. Society has been taught that men are the dominant sex and gender, thus making them and their "assigned qualities" more desired.
>
> The problem is not when you express your own preferences or wishes but when you can only define that you are okay with your own preferences by contrasting them against some other thing that you then insist MUST be lesser and inferior. The problem is with a social system where misogyny is so deeply embedded that men wield it against other men and themselves.

There are some truths to these statements, and the struggle to be "a man" comes from the behaviors we were taught growing up: the "men take care of the wife, men provide, and men protect" idealism. This is sexual segregation at its finest. I've seen women be equally those things, if not more. I ran into an article that expressed an amazing thought. It suggested an attempt to live without limitations, without any preconceived ideas about what might be best for me. For one, most people enjoy being surprised; two, living without the constraints is a better way to live. I remember reading a quote that masculinity has nothing to do with mannerisms and the like, but mostly is transmitted through winning battles through honor and nobility. For some reason, that resonated so deeply through my conscious mind and even more importantly to my heart and soul.

Rico Suave:
Putting His Best Foot Forward

Flirting can be defined as how to engage someone without making something seem uncomfortable or awkward. There's a fine line there, and often, most stutter at the thought of creating the best first impression possible. The art of flirting is a skill, and you should stop feeling like your flirting game is optimal on a digital dating platform. Just like riding a bike, you can't expect to be good at it on the first go-around. Chances are, if you are bad at flirting, you are bad at dating. There is a symbiotic relationship, and I apologize in advance. Initial chemistry is something I can't measure as a matchmaker. I can hear and note the client's type, but sometimes I have matched people that are each other's physical types to the tee, but the chemistry just wasn't there. It's totally normal, and there is nothing we can do. Onward we go, right?

To jump-start the connection process, there's a way to be classy, cute, and witty at the same time in regard to flirtation. Don't be drunk and don't be high. This sounds so blatant for me to say, but I must say it out loud. If you really need those things to loosen up, they have medication a doctor can diagnose and prescribe to you professionally. A lot of my friends on those medications are some of the best people I know, so no judgment at all. I am a big fan of playful sarcasm and banter. I also like one simple shoulder grab, but you're only allowed a couple on date one or two. A guy I dated once told me that he liked the way I smelled, and I replied, "I showered just for you, that's probably why." He then responded something along the lines of "Thanks for doing it for me." A guy once ran up to me after I was about to leave a holiday party and asked if he could walk me to my car in the cold. He got a date out of me. Simplicity is key! You see? Something quick, cute, and unexpected—that's all you need. The more you think like every other LA gay man, the more you're treated as one. In this instance, not going against the grain has an implication of you being boring, especially in a creative town like LA, where everything is about being in a niche and being original. Good news is that we can sometimes hide behind a personal connection through dating applications or dating online in general. Messaging doesn't define true subtext or importance, but if you are in the flesh, let the eye contact, a genuine smile, and a little moment of silence do the work for you. A smile says a lot. It's your secret weapon. Think about the last time you were in the grocery store and someone smiled at you. It kind of is startling and unsolicited in LA to have a stranger be genuinely kind to you, but where I was raised, down South, a smile is something contagious. I want to try and start a revolution here in the world, do you care to join?

Having a gal pal wing woman always helps. She is your secret tactic with her boobs. Not be politically incorrect, of course. They are always better and less threatening than your other gay brothers. However, don't be so close to her that she is actually preventing you from dating on your own and vice versa. A friend of mine had to divorce her best gay friend because they were becoming a couple, without being an official couple. Now, they are both married, separately. Your gal pal can start a conversation with someone you find cute at a bar, and then you kinda "join in," as opposed to it being something that might be seen as overwhelming initially. It's like she takes the "what should I say to him first" awkwardness away. It's almost as if you can observe and feel the attraction out from afar without actually talking to that person. Then, you can casually chime in if the chemistry seems right, and if so, you'll probably slowly make your way to it just being a conversation between the both of you. Hopefully, your girlfriend doesn't mind being the third wheel. I was always very lucky with mine. They would always find someone else to talk to or would find the one straight man in the gay bar.

Communication is also very sexy. If someone offers to take you out on a date, and you can't for whatever reason, you return the favor, and if you want extra brownie points, with an actual phone call.

I cannot tell you how that immediately sends people into optimal flirtation outer space. Initiative is sexy, and never forget that. It's all about that appeal sometimes without even hearing a person speak. Without it, the date will always die, and that date that seemed so promising will never happen. The little things are actually the bigger things that set you apart from everyone else. Be unordinary, and always put your best foot forward. If things never worked out with someone, I always knew I tried to put my best foot forward, regardless of circumstance. I am a huge promoter of getting back to people in a timely manner. Mind you, my phone isn't glued to me, and it's not like I am incessantly on it. Instead of making him understand why you haven't texted him in six hours, give him value and let him know in advance that you are unplugged. But seriously, how many people on this earth are away from their phones for more than a few hours? It's sad but realistic. Maybe you are seeing a long movie, are in back to back meetings for hours, or traveling, but there is still a responsibility you have to give yourself to keep the ball rolling. Isn't it so strange for a person nowadays to say, "I haven't been on my phone all day." Um, I smell bullshit. Of course you have. You just checked in via social media at Target because you got in to get two things and you came out with twelve. My motto is that if you have time to pee, you have time to text someone. If I can work a seventeen-hour workday and get back to everyone in a timely manner, you can too, my friend. I've had many guys who "were very busy" for several weeks after introducing them to someone initially, even when they implored that they "were ready to date." They would start the e-mail like, "Mason, sorry for not getting back to you sooner. He must think I am such a flake." Yes, he does, and I do too, if I am being unfiltered. Accountability and setting up the date yourself, taking the reins, can be used to ward off this particular label: just do it!

Sometimes I get the question of when the best time is for the infamous first kiss. I say, if the chemistry is great, the comfort level is there, I say date one! Go for it! I find that if the date was really good, it's confusing not to do it to the other person. Plus, we gay men are more physical beings, and there's nothing more startling than a person who loves kissing your nostrils instead of your lips or simply biting your lips until they bleed. Not speaking from experience, of course. Basically, don't be a prude, but don't be a sloppy slut either. It will always remain an awkward exchange after your first date when you two leave the restaurant. If anything, just ask, "Can I kiss you?" What is he going to say? I doubt a gay man will say no if your intuitive nature guides you efficiently. Sometimes that can be a telltale sign if there will be a next time. Something mysterious can be extremely successful down the line. Leave the lion hungry for another meal, per se. Let him know he's attractive, which feels nice enough, via a simple peck. If it's a maybe, wait. No need to force anything. Let that be the dessert for next time.

It never hurts to have a bit of street-smarts too, let's face it. It's imperative for us to really get to know someone, in person. A person can sound amazing on paper, can look unbelievably handsome in a photo, but our attraction has to come from an internal and physical standpoint. This is the only way to see if there's active and receptive flirtation in front of you. The most success in preliminary dating happens when someone meets someone else in-person, and sooner rather than later. Also, when a person takes initiative and communicates fluidly. It's the proverbial glue to all relationships. Without an adhesive, you are going down a damning slippery slope. There is an unbelievably undeniable drop in interest if nothing happens within a fourteen-day period. Do yourself a favor and compliment him if your life is overly preoccupied at the moment. Do you like him? Tell him. Do you think you just got a friend vibe? Tell him. I tell men all the time that they are nice, but I don't feel the physical chemistry. It is in the minority to do this, so don't be like everyone else if you have spent more than three to five dates with this person. Honesty is the best and sometimes the worst thing you can get from someone, but at least you know a solid response. I was always so appreciative when someone told me they weren't interested: "I know you're a busy guy, so I wanted to let you know that although I think you're a great guy, I'm not sure it's a match, so it's probably better we don't meet Friday. I wish you well, though, cutie." On another account, I got a text from this one guy before that said, "I would totally sleep with you, but I just don't think we're a good match." He gave me the worst backhanded compliment ever, right? He felt I was attractive, but we shouldn't waste our time because there was no emotional connection. Gray area usually means no, unfortunately, in my book. I get frustrated with this "when to text and not text" scenario. It's stupid, and please throw it out the window while it's on fire. Everyone likes a honeymoon phase, and remind yourself how easy it was to see the person you liked because you made the time. It's irritating to me to see such a strong match go to waste, where flirtation rules were being honored, just by bad first impressions alone, and molasses-like daters. If everyone wanted to be pursued, we'd have a very lonely world. No one wants to feel like they are driving the ship anymore. I will take the reins for a couple of days after a good first date. On the other hand, if I am fifty-fifty on someone and they initiate the conversation, almost always I will take the leap and do something casual. First introductions shouldn't be the main gauge for how attraction is initially in the fifty-fifty world. I've been on and set up many dates over the years that were, in fact, pleasant surprises. I usually feel everything out on a case-by-case basis. I am pretty good about instigating a morning greeting and creating active communication during the day in the beginning. Sometimes, I get in the habit of feeling not wanted or desired, and I simply stop caring. I think to myself, *He's probably just not into me, and that's okay.* I usually follow a forty-eight-hour rule. I mean, telling me I'm handsome in person is one thing, and me noticing the solid flirtation, but your compliments are pleasant, but mean nothing until you take the time to flirt with me when the time is less convenient. You have to date smart, be open, but don't be so open where you can start feeling tired of dating and let down—it's about balance.

Over the long-term, things you can't measure can multiply your chances for dating success. Enough focusing on their monetary or their education clout, really pay attention to things that matter most for the purposes of longevity. Generosity, integrity, humility, and kindness go a long way when you are trying to build that fire when you meet someone. Be the person that leaves an impact on someone else about who you are as "just a good person," as opposed to someone who ranted off this material bribery. "I like that you called me before we met. It's refreshing." I remember hearing that many times from guys I've dated in the past. It took just an ounce of kindness to develop a pound of positive result: a little flirtation that wasn't as physical. Your talking does nothing when we can't see you physically walking. If he ain't gonna give you time, he ain't worth a dime.

The Switch

I meet all sorts of people at all ages, at all points of life. When the verbiage focus goes from attraction—"I want him to be Caucasian, stocky. I prefer this sexual position"—to "I just want a man whom I can come home to and who would treat me well, that I can see a solid future with," I know that the switch cranks have started turning. When someone can decipher between a man who is genetically handsome as an inheritance from someone who is internally attractive, and has done their work. When the threshold of unambiguous position preferences start to diminish, these men seek pleasure in exploration, which presents some vibrancy and spontaneity in a relationship. This model is very true to gay men who want monogamous, long-term relationships. I have my own different opinion about open relationships where this model might not apply completely. Do you really want the person you fall in love with to be the best sex you have had? Sometimes that "best sex" can develop once a true, genuine connection is established. Ask yourself, do you want to go home with someone, or do you wish to make a home with someone one day? On average, I see this process mostly happen around early to midthirties in a gay man. Then, there are those men I have met who have been ready at twenty-five, and then other men over forty-five that still feel like they are in their glory days. The older party animals don't normally make it to our office space anyway. In conversations to help me identify men that have made this transition, certain words begin to become more winsome and less physical.

We gay men can sometimes be guilty of dating in reverse. You know, when we hook up with someone without knowing too much about them, and then we give ourselves permission to get to know someone on a more elevated level. I am not one to talk because I have done this a handful of times. Sometimes a great first date can turn into something physical by the end of the evening because of the need of physical chemistry confirmation. That is one piece of the puzzle for us gay men that acts as a strong indicator of our primal instinct: to mate. I found the men I've been in relationships that reverted to this behavior went away quickly rather than stay, though. People would simply disappear and never call me back. Maybe the thrill and mystery of exploring someone's physical body was more definite and engaging than the internal attraction. However, physicality and sexual chemistry isn't enough. Once we've let go of that mystery, sometimes one can throw his hands up and realize this act may be "as good as it will get." I have seen it work, though, and the relationship and excitement build organically. In that case, go for it, but just make sure you both are on the same page about where you are in regard to relationship timelines, and this is past date one. Leave the goo-goo eyes at home, and take a tiny sip of realism.

One of my fellow matchmakers said, "My new client was like, 'I am miserable because all these models and actors don't have a personality, and I'm only attracted to them.'" This man sounds like an addict to me. He keeps doing the same thing and expects a different result. I can't take a shower. My fear has dissipated significantly, but I've muted the feeling of fear so much over the years, that is nearly nonexistent, which makes me a better shower-er. Reason being, when I was little, a centipede crawled out of the water spicket and was swimming like a gigantic, vicious serpent in the water, while I froze in pure panic. It affected my entire life, and it's something that will probably never go away. It's hard for me to revert to not looking down when I first go into the shower. With men like this who go through circumstances that change them, I see that he has his hand on the crank of our proverbial switch, but sometimes he may need a mentor of some kind to give him a helping hand to ignite that internal validation and rotation. As a matchmaker, you are paying me to make you accountable by being punctual, honest, and willing to take constructive criticism. Do a quick Rolodex check of your friends. How many of them are willing to have an uncomfortable conversation with you? The LA "Hi, how are you?" welcome can be monotonous, robotic, and empty at times. It's simply annoying to me. But *really*, how are you? Don't be scared to challenge someone you know well, and be appreciative when someone does it to you. It's a mere sign of admiration and projected, positive growth, and not a sign of character defamation. Someone asked me how my day was, and I just laid it on the line, unfiltered. I was going through a tough time in the winter of one year, and the person I told said, "You'd never know you were dealing with so much. You have way more grace than most folks I know." For me, I wasn't fishing for a compliment, but it just felt good to let it out and make the feeling transparent. Old Mason would have just smiled and nodded and given an operative two-word answer: "I'm good." People ask me because they want to know. They aren't just saying that just to be nice and fill the room with an audible voice rather than awkward silence. If they are close to me, they deserve to know about my general well-being.

As a professional sleuth, I try to perpetuate the switch as much as I am able. People can come in and out of this too. Some people turn it off once they have felt they have fulfilled a partnership piece. Meaning, a person who was in a relationship for ten years might not be in the hugest rush to be a devoted partner again right away. This can be a scary thing. I remember working with a client who hadn't dated in many years. Keep in mind, dating in 2000 was much different than dating in this present day and age. I think he spent years convincing himself that he was unattractive and crowded his life with fillers rather than dealing with his true demons, which was his self-confidence. He dug himself quite a self-destructing hole over time. As his matchmaker, I needed to let him know that he was enough and start building him stairs above sea level. He should stop doing comparisons, but should give himself permission to mess up a lot along the way and to not get too defeated. When we were younger, we all fell on our bikes many times before we actually became experts. Seems like he was still aching from a few skinned knees, which impeded his switch.

Obviously, I only work with men that make themselves open to the idea of change. I refuse to force someone to be a certain way if they are not ready or need a little time to be ready. There were many times in my matchmaking career where I bit my tongue way too many times where I wish I didn't. Sometimes, when you work for a company, there is always a business element to things. Of course, I don't try to rush the switch, but I get that some people really need to feel liberated and unrestrained, and by that, I mean have safe, responsible sex with trusted partners until you realize that the physical is less than transcendental. Then, after they've had their fun, we can have our realistic powwow.

Where I feel the most confusion in dating occurs when a guy presents himself on the progressive side of the switch but really isn't ready. It's almost the premise of proposed and surface expectations in conjunction with false advertising. These men love to paint this grandiose portrait of wanting something long-term, but it's really something on a canvas that is cheap, more black-and-white, with a lead pencil, and that took five minutes. Which is a perfectly acceptable period to be in, but then the other guy feels like he just "wasted his time." I wouldn't define it as a true waste, but it is a little frustrating to spend time with a man who misrepresents himself in any sense when the other man is being forthright.

I see timelines also as a big indication for which seems invigorating versus intimidating to some people. I told this one fella on a dating application that there wasn't any initial chemistry between us after we had switched photos. I was quite sad because he seemed so great on paper, but I told him I didn't have a lot of free time, and I need *just* enough initial chemistry to allow myself to be excited and have that chemistry grow further, hopefully in person. I told him that I wanted a husband in five years. This also was my dry, sarcastic humor speaking. He responded with "That's quite the timeline." Really? I am twenty-eight years old, and having a partner by thirty-three seems intimidating and unreasonable? By the standards of Southern roots, I am a disappointing anomaly. I should have had two kids by now, with a house and a white picket fence. Oh, and then there's me not being straight. Gay men are so distant when it comes to parameters. Gay men never want to feel confined in a way. Gay men who are near or practicing the switch know their boundaries and are realistic. There's a big difference in having standards and expectations rather than liking the idea of them. Some people might argue that these types of men are "too much too soon." However, I'd rather someone be upfront and honest than to play this ring-around-the-roses game that leads to nowhere and have my time wasted.

I was talking to one of my friends about the idea of emotional security. He had broken up with a guy that he felt was emotionally dependent on him. This comes from the lack of emotionally stable backgrounds in the ideal of family mentorship. My friend confirmed that he didn't have the optimal family that showed emotional complacency. These types of men have tunnel vision, not seeing both sides of the emotional spectrum. As humans, we must survey what's not only in front of us, but also to our left and right: a 360-degree view. Gay men who aren't harboring the switch aren't able to facilitate the responsibility of emotional normalcy. This is by trial and error, and this panoramic viewpoint comes from mistakes and just dating experience in general.

Ask yourself, where do you think you lie in the spectrum of this theory? Do you have considerate friends placing their hands on this switch on top of yours? Will you continue to wander in the dark and try to figure things out on your own? Sometimes building change is much more rewarding than letting things happen organically.

Pick Up, Start Again

Rain gives us a sense of renewal. I remember having one of the worst holiday seasons of my life. Discovered cancers, deaths of dear loved ones, hospitalizations, and a lost love, all in a thirty-day period. Happy holidays. Before heading east to visit my family, I remember this dreary, cold rain. I felt I needed a grounding yoga class before the hustle and bustle of the holidays began, and I arrived early to decompress a little. There was this point right before class where I was able to see the dusk build itself in an array of thick clouds. My nose tickled with nostalgia, loving the smell of wet concrete I grew to know too well during my childhood. It was that moment that I knew that I was going to be okay. That the wheel of our personal world goes on smooth paths, cobblestone ones, and then ones that might stick in the mud a little. At the end of the day, there's a progression forward.

Mercury Retrograde was in its most active audible roar after that same holiday period. I'm not sure how much I believe in something so intangible and ethereal, but it seemed to resonate with me so well more so than ever. I was dealing with so many changes: someone I was currently dating and also five close friends who all had broken up with their significant others of six months or more. I wanted to be that solid rock for them, but it honestly felt like I was a clump of hardened sand that could disintegrate at the drop of any sense of moisture. All those individuals are amazing people who live through their truth and heart. Most of them had been living with their other half, had been talking about them getting married, or even having the convincing talk that the person was *the one*. It was devastating for all of them, and it was hard to see someone so great become so lonely and small. It's like nursing a very sore muscle. It doesn't get better by just sitting there. I remember telling this to one of those individuals. It's important to funnel these feelings of despair into something creative, productive, and maybe just distracting for a short while. I've always noticed that a lot of relationships follow a distinctive pattern. Over the years, I have many mentors allude to this kind of timeline. You have the first three months, where it's all just about skipping and holding hands, making plans, and being all annoyingly jovial and all that jazz. Then, from the three-to-six-month period, you start noticing behavioral and thought patterns in someone and start being comfortable with being more honest and less guarded. During this period, there is a lot of conversation of noticing habits and coming to a point of negotiation. Between the six-and-nine-month period is the make it or break it period. This is the point where true character becomes apparent, and you notice habits that actually may never change, so you have to start a conversation of compromise that is fair for both parties to be able to sustain normalcy without having anything feel like a burden of some kind. Do you agree with this timeline based on your own personal experiences?

As gay men, when we come to moments where we are at our lowest, we tend to allow things to escalate until they avalanche. We can be a little more emotional than our straight male counterparts. Of course, this can go for anyone, but a lot of things can be stigmas in what we have dealt with as gay men in the past, like acceptance, being comfortable as we are, and intimacy. "Gosh, I need to lose ten pounds," "I need to be ten years younger," "I need to, I need to…" To be honest, you shouldn't have to change for anyone unless you know it's going to benefit your personal health both physically and emotionally down the line. Sometimes, as a reminder, there are things in our character that we must tweak to allow us to be receptive fully in the pure sense of who we are.

Sometimes I wonder, am I writing my own story, or am I being the blank piece of paper and my potential the writing instrument? I started to realize that this concept can come from a place of sadness and that the canvas needs to feel like the other person can inspire him and contribute in some way. Sometimes the mourning lover has the pen in his hand, hands it over, and wants the other to take action to write their happy ending together. In continuation with this dynamic, whenever this happens in relationships, one person always starts resenting the other. One person feels like one person is obliviously gliding by, and the other party is internally exhausted. Fear and sadness are sources of resentment. Everyone deserves to be nurtured in some way, which can serve as the catalyst of this ideal.

I performed an informal survey on breakup statistics. I informally polled 107 single gay men across the country, ages twenty-five to fifty. Obviously, these predictions would be a little more accurate if I had surveyed ten times the amount. In reviewing my results, I noticed that nearly half of these relationships had ended because of a communication issue or some form of lying. The act of cheating was inclusive in this category of being dishonest. *Lying* constituted of a relationship that might have opened and failed, which normally transitioned into some form of infidelity. In third place, there was a direct tie between gay men feeling like their initial fire in the relationship slowly dwindled over time (I found that most men also said that they were still platonic and friendly if they were in this category) and then proximity issues. This could mean that the potential simply moved away, and long-distance correspondence failed, or the other party felt like the other person created a lot of physical distance from a lack of work and life balance. All the other categories only made up 24 percent collectively. Can you say you were part of this surveyed majority? I wouldn't leave out the other reasons, which were things like in the minority of this study, like addictive and abusive behaviors or identity issues. The more understanding you are of the reasons why relationships fail, the more aware you should be of your own actions and personal flow. A lot of the more minimal categories were also paired with other slivers of the pie in an obvious fashion; meaning, men with destructive behavior also were not faithful in their own relationships. I found it very unsurprising that communication and lying were the popular reasons of breakups. Generally, if you are not communicating in a relationship, the other party feels like you are not invested fully and starts having very damning internal conversations. You can see that from this study, the odds are in your favor if you communicate effectively, basically, eliminating 50 percent of the reasons on why your potential relationship would be flushed down the drain.

There are ways to prevent certain behaviors if you eliminate the infamous gray area in the beginning. Trust me, passive convincing goes a long way here. Then again, I'm finding that more gay men want to be chased, and when the chaser fails, they become the person who wants to be pursued from the lack of positive reinforcement. As a reminder, you communicate more than you know without even speaking.

On the surface, there is nothing good about breakups, but they get much easier as time passes, which is the only true way to heal appropriately. They all come in their own shapes, sizes, and intensity. I absolutely love my job, but sadly, I hear more horror and suspense stories rather than fantasies where "dreams come true," and you "live happily ever after." Why would someone come to me when things seem all peachy with sunsets and rainbows? It's my job to provide a safety net for individuals and provide insight on thought processes. At the end of the day, people think they are unique, but certain situations seem distinctly similar from a more grandiose viewpoint. Life brings us situations that can change us for the better or for the worse. I want my audience to know that I am human too, that I don't have a perfect love life, because I think being a "love doctor," people think I should be the person who always has a significant other or be able to diagnose and heal problems quickly. In fact, the matchmaker mindset is relatively shut off in most of my personal dating practices. Surgeons have to shut it off when they have seen three individuals die in front of them in a small span of time. I'd rather things be organic instead of the natural flow being impeded by a personal, nitpicky thought process, something I preach and advocate to my clientele. People would also presume that I must be picky. I actually am pretty open, but I am picky with the integrity a man holds himself to, and that can be a rarer find. I have come to the conclusion that I give myself so many rules and regulations, and for no reason. I should trust that I am a good person and that people will understand that if I am not the solid, perfect, professional entrepreneur picture I am trying so intricately to paint all the time, I'll be okay. Ask yourself, what rules and regulations do you put on yourself that impede your growth potential? Sometimes I can be in my head, though, like any normal person. I get scared and frustrated all the time in my own dating life. I understand that I grow more through things that I attribute as negative than when things are positive all the time. I want to be known for practicing what I preach. That's important to me and in the model of business I conduct.

There was a relationship I'll refer to where the breakup punch knocked me down with a big KO. It had everything in the beginning: chemistry, compassion, conversation, and understanding. I could go on and on about it. Someone told me once that relationships should be like a bank; there's an equal deposit and withdraw on both ends. I felt we had that, especially in the beginning. I still smile when I think about how amazing this relationship was to me. The thing, though, about dating men that can start having selfish and narcissistic behaviors, where people like me get caught up in it, is that they will have $100, but deposit $99 to the other party and still be happy with just $1. Years ago, I had some tragic events happen to me that threatened my health over the course of an entire year. I am thankfully in great health now, but through that process, I became unafraid of fearing death anymore. It was a defining moment that hasn't been forgotten, even to this current day. I told myself that I would now forever have my heart open. I would live in peace as much as I can. I will live life with no regrets and not be afraid to expose a man to what I can offer to him sooner rather than later, in the most genteel way possible. In the course of the time we shared together, our relationship started to slowly dwindle. I'm not a person who will explosively argue, so our conversations seemed pretty normative in the sense of challenging a normal relationship. Maybe it was a lot of me trying to convince myself that it was going to work, and in fact, that was one of the last things he had said to me, that I "wanted this relationship to work so bad." I have a tendency to do that, to change things about myself before I even ask my partner. On a long-term scale, keeping silent for so long can feel quite defeating to one's personal authenticity. I have always been maternal like that in my personal life, caring for people and easily being able to sacrifice my own behaviors to make our relationship better. I realized that I was depositing so much in this relationship that I felt like I went bankrupt. Once I realized this,

I was able to look at myself in the contents from tl
relationship. Then, I was able to identify that I shoul
is listening to me, no matter what, and never questio
unless it were to do harm to myself. My cup felt hal
time.

Through all of the fog in our relationship, the bad timing of
our lives, the things that stand out to me the most is the fact that I
never thought he respected me although his love for me was something that I never questioned. I remember reading a horoscope that
said, "Once you feel you can't respect someone, you are done with
them." This is 100 percent accurate, and this goes for any kind of
relationship label. He was on a turbulent roller-coaster ride, and I
was on a smooth, repetitive merry-go-round. He was slightly older
and more "ahead of his game," but I felt he never saw me truly as
his equal, because I felt there were many, similar parallels to our
relationship. Our relationship seemed perpendicular rather than
having a very steady, linear trajectory. Obviously, his past long-term
relationship had given him demons he was working through, which
was normal. We all have them, though. Secondly, he had an issue
with accountability. Throughout the course of our relationship, he
might have admitted he was wrong maybe twice. Instead of taking
ownership, he would blame other individuals for not thinking like
him: a difference between a scared boy and an honorable man. This
could be seen as very selfish, although I felt like he could choose
to be a very selfless lover. I shouldn't place all the blame on him,
because we all know it takes two to tango, and he could probably
say a number of things about my communication style, but lessons
learned all around.

So then I am here now. A stronger gay man who is now a different gay man. A friend of mine told me, "Mason, you are so close
to finding the one that was meant for you, look at all the growth you
have achieved the past three years [as a gay man]. I am proud of you."
So I now can remove myself from that relationship and look at it as
a chance to grow and learn for a better future. "Relationships should
be that easy, Mason. Take it from me, a forty-year-old woman who
is now just getting married for the first time," another friend added.

Studies have shown that it take eight weeks for a person to stop going from logical thought to emotional thinking rapidly in the case of a breakup. This is a mere average, of course. Some can take a couple of years to get over, if the relationship was fairly long. There was a similar study that noted how seeing a picture of an ex after a breakup can activate an area of the brain that is linked with cocaine addiction and physical pain, which can suggest that heartbreak can actually feel like physical pain or even drug withdrawal. That crazy, stress-releasing hormone cortisol can do crazy things to us anatomically. That's why when we break up with someone, our thoughts seem like they are so discombobulated. When I was working for a more elite, heterosexual clientele base, my boss at that time and I would talk about this one client that we would reject continuously because he hadn't successfully debonded from his previous girlfriend. They were together for many years. He would constantly say he was ready, but the energy exchange between him and my boss seemed otherwise. The detox can be painstaking. Heartbreak is something that everyone goes through. For the personal relationship I was referring to prior, I can remember being in my apartment by myself after we had talked as lovers for the last time and looking at all the sweet love letters he wrote me on my kitchen bulletin board, not being able to see them from the amount of tears that were trickling down my cheeks. I kept repeating to myself over and over again, "I can't look at these anymore." Devastation. Agony. I was a shell of emptiness, completely numb. The most I had cried since my grandfather's death years ago. I was so appreciative of some friends that came over and made me chocolate pudding.

A friend told me that a colleague or mentor told her that if things hindered her happiness, she should just throw it out. She always noticed this wine rack an old boyfriend had given her years ago, and she thought that every time she saw it, it would immediately bring her back to that relationship. She felt there was so much more value in the evacuation, and it brought her more of a sense of a cleansing of her space. Needless to say, I had to just throw everything away I was given by most of my exes. I've had that happen to me as well. One guy literally brought me one of my baseball-style shirt when we said our good-byes. I honestly get it. It felt bittersweet on both ends, I imagine, but it was necessary.

I was involved in a shorter, three-month relationship that will forever also leave a place in my heart. It's funny how life sends us certain individuals to make a certain change, whether they initially have the appeal of enlightenment or coming from a tumultuous nature. I met him from another, newer dating application that my girlfriend suggested, where she met her significant other at that time. I first met him for happy hour on the same day I had met another guy for a second date, who later disappeared. You do what you gotta do to not be a crazy cat lady who's single her whole life. I stuck with him, and we both agreed not to see anyone else after two weeks of dating each other. He was slightly older and lived very far away. Sometimes I would spend two hours in the car to see him when he was only twenty miles away. Oh, LA, and your traffic. I really liked him and didn't mind at first. He had the most amazing, supportive friends and family. I really loved that about him. I was quickly introduced to all of them. Over time, I felt like my feelings were getting hurt or my emotional needs were not being met. I felt I was putting in 80 percent in our relationship. In three months, he met one or two of my friends (one for ten minutes before my yoga class), he spent the night with me three or four times, and then he thanked me once for driving down to see him. He told me I was handsome and that he liked me maybe two or three times total. I had bought him flowers, made him cards of appreciation, organized a surprise birthday for him, gotten to know his story, and was just an overall trustworthy person for him. He supported me at one of my work events, and I returned the favor. The dam felt too full on my end, though. I wasn't in that "keeping tabs" mind-set, until I looked at everything from a bird's-eye view. I wrote him an e-mail that clearly noted the behaviors he was doing that made me feel like I was number 5 on his list, that everything was easy to him because it was convenient for him. You would think that I would think he was selfish, but he had such an inherent, loving nature about him that I never thought of that for one second. I was shattered to hear that he knew I deserved better. He told me I was a good person. I gave him gratitude for being a kind person. I really wanted us to work, and that potential put a big chip on my shoulder for a while. He couldn't provide me things that told me that this was a team effort, and he told me that he "couldn't do" what I asked of him because his "life is just that way it is now." I just wanted a compliment every once in a while and for him to invite me to things as opposed to assuming that I was invited. There's a stark difference. I wasn't asking much. I wasn't able to tell him that he lived in a relationship-convenient world, and a lot of guys would feel like he didn't care over time. It's not my responsibility anyway. I was just a bit shocked since he himself and one of his close friends told me he was serious about building something long-term with someone. I remember reading his profile again after we had broken up, and he wanted someone who didn't play games, would make him laugh, and would let him know that someone was interested in him. I can say I did all those things successfully. He did check in with me every day, which he knew I appreciated. He just didn't bother to fuse himself with my life, because I made the best effort to infuse mine to his. It wasn't even until I stepped away before I actually looked selfishly at my own needs and wants. I remember him making jokes with a hidden meaning about how I wasn't his "friend" on Facebook. I had listened to my heart center on this one, because I felt no rush to do so. My social media page is a clear representation of my friends and the love and appreciation they have for me and how the effort stems from myself as well. It seemed like he wanted to get to know them on a very surface level—another convenient outlet for him—because he made no tangible effort to know them on a personal one. I made so many sacrifices that I felt went unnoticed, and I think he didn't initially make many sacrifices for me. He didn't even get a chance to hear my entire story; he only saw a glimmer, and that was my only regret. With this regret, it's not of my own accord but on me wishing he had asked or showed enough to care to know. He said he wanted to be friends, and I could see that, but not in the near future. I felt my bond of trust was broken, and it would take a lot for me to find that cement again.

I remember having a bad nightmare just days after I had broken up with this same individual. It was alarming, but it spearheaded my deepest fear: betrayal. This is something that was a blast from my past from previous breakups, and this made it so apparent to me more so than ever. It was lingering in my subconscious, and it finally made itself known in full transparency. I remember being in something like an old train station with wooden pews. My "boyfriend" stood there, in front of everyone, looked at me, and made this speech that made me feel very belittled, isolated, and worthless. Although he never did that in actuality, I remember feeling as if my face were melting from all the moisture rolling down it. I kept thinking, *After all that I did for him.* I just remember aimlessly going through the train station, trying to get people to listen to me, but I was left shunned, ignored, and still devastated. I came out of that experience not jaded but empowered, more aware, and stronger. Never will I second-guess what I need and deserve in a partnership. Never will I agree to condescension, but only with a soul of openness and warmth. Never will I doubt how much I can offer someone in confidence rather than in the act of arrogance or blame. I would want my partner to want all these things from me as well.

Can you say that you love yourself just as you are? Close your eyes and imagine your perfect man. Los Angeles or any bigger metropolitan city can be treacherous to navigate, but you deserve nothing less than the dream man you want, with all the feasible and realistic bells and whistles. No one is perfect. There will be some compromises, but are those coming from a place of admiration or a place of someone feeling like their character is being defamed? See this as a process of redemption and hope rather than an endless feeling of despair and defeat. Through your battle wounds come scars that serve as tattoos of remembrance, where you were and where you want to be in your future. Be a warrior, and don't be afraid to face your fears.

My thing I always tell my friends is this: *If you feel like you can now be rejected, be vulnerable to love, you can start dating again.* In order for you to be loved, you have to love yourself first. Rejection is difficult. Even I've been rejected, and many times. However, after a while, I saw that as an opportunity to really chisel the man I wanted to be and the man I wanted to be with. You'll know a person is worth that third or fourth date when the process becomes intimidating, maybe scary. One of the most rewarding things about my job is that I am able to sit with someone I might have exchanged a couple of e-mails with, and they immediately feel like I had been their best friend. They instantly trust me without feeling judged or ashamed. Maybe it's because they figured I have seen and heard it all, which is possibly true. They tell me the nitty gritty, their pasts that have shaped them, and that only allows my analysis of them to be truer and more authentic. I really encourage my clients to do that on a date, being vulnerable with some feasible and understandable parameters. I wouldn't say bring a dozen red roses on the second or third date, but really allow the other person to see what your heart is saying and how that conversation can be unspoken and absorbed organically. Take the high road and be ahead of the game rather than him asking you first.

I always love telling the story of a day I ran into a very chi-chi coffee shop for a meeting. I grabbed my cup of joe, had my meeting, and then needed another pick-me-up before I left. I had asked for the refill price, and the lady gladly gave me it. Before I knew it, we were talking because of her engrained positive attitude. When I left, she told me the price, and I quickly nodded and left. When checking my receipt, I noticed she forgot to charge me the refill price. I found this completely odd because I agreed to it, and she should have caught it. Here's my lesson: it didn't matter what she charged because I was so enamored by her zest for life. I was drawn into her spell without even realizing it. I immediately thought, *This is how I can be a better dater, by looking at life in such a positive light and allowing my happiness to reflect in my character and present essence.* As hokey as it seems, if you want to blow your date out of the water, you must do it with a chivalrous effort. When dating on my own, I always got the comment of, "You are not like most LA guys." I'm like, probably not. I'm usually on time, never flake, will pay for our meal equally, and will open the door for you. How is this out of the norm, and shouldn't this be a given?

So what happens after you break up with him and you want to be friends again? It's quite a vulnerable and highly sensitive time for both parties, both physically and emotionally, and words can be said that can easily be misconstrued. The majority of the time (I see this in relationships under the one-year mark, especially), being friends with your ex is probable but unlikely. I am not one to believe in astrological theories, but as a Leo, I will say, once I realize that we aren't compatible in any further form, I am done with you. Done, done. I am cordial, but there is a hard stop after being a gentleman in a social setting. After all, you probably shared mutual friends, and you would be bound to run into each other again at some point. However, I will say if I am not done, I'll be a great friend to you. One of my close gay friends told me that I am "good about doing that." However, I just saw a recent article claiming if people do this too often, they are sociopaths. Go figure. There are some exes that I have amazing relationships with, and some that we realized our personalities would never mesh, no matter how hard we try, and it's better that we don't speak anymore. Sometimes I see them as needing to realize things about themselves before we can talk again. Whatever you do, once you have profoundly debonded from your past mate, do not be physical with them ever again. Doing that will just cause the worse unexpected riptide in your emotional stability and give you failed expectations. Doing so will just leave you in a pussy mess after you remove your bandage. I did that once before, and I wanted to punch him before our initial breakup, and after, I thought we could "try again." I should have learned that placing my hand on a hot stove would give me the same scalding result. We've all been there, right?

I remember an amazing seven-month relationship, and he looked me in the face the day we broke up and told me he would basically never talk to me again. This breakup was very amicable, or at least I thought. He literally deleted me from his life in every way possible. I thought this was a bit harsh, but I guess it was what he needed, and his own truth is something I will always admire. Everyone has his own learning curve. I will say, this is quite the hard thing to do for the younger generation of gays. The older gays are just more mature, and we youngsters should take a heavy note. You can only be friends with exes if both of you are evenly matched; meaning, both parties have a significant other of some sort, and a considerable amount of time has elapsed. I haven't had much success outside of that formula. If one guy has found another catch and the other is still single, you can see that the parallels in conversation can be quite uneven and awkward.

Here's a good metaphor. It's kind of like how when you were in college or currently in your workplace environment when you were assigned a project in a team environment. You had *that* person in your group that may have done nothing or just contributed bumps in the road to the success of a good grade. After that experience, you made a valiant effort to never work with them again, right? Same with relationships and breakups. Once you realize that your thought processes are way too different, you realize there is no point in trying again, otherwise you might be getting the same ominous result. Sometimes, it's just best to let things go, see them as they are, and move on.

I have a way with words. For me, whenever I want to be sound and astute in a relationship that is veering to a halt or a slower pace, I have to write it down. For some reason, my fears and emotional hindrances are being drawn out from my soul and being placed on paper. These letters should come more from a logical sense rather than an emotional one. I've seen myself mostly doing this after the three month mark of me dating someone. I submit a request to the person I have been dating, and then we're both able to sit back and realize what we want and don't want in a partnership. After the submission of this "letter," I know that I have said my peace, and followed my truth, and it's our opportunity as a "couple" to either let things be, or start comprising and explore that next stage in the relationship. End with a sense of gratitude rather than sense of animosity. For straight people, I assume this is probably what a woman does passively if she wants marriage and wants to start moving forward to the white picket fence life she has always dreamed to have.

A friend of a friend recently gave me this advice, and it really resonated with me: "I believe the focus should be always on 'Who treats me/gives me what I expect and want' rather than 'How can I make this work because I like the person?'" Another friend of mine recently mentioned to me that "expectations are past failures." I got to thinking about it, and it's kind of true. You know, turning lemons into lemonade, learning from our mistakes. We expect certain behaviors from someone because the opposite behaviors elicited a negative response in us prior. This is where fear can permeate through us. We get burned, and then we sometimes feel, "Is this all that I deserve?" or we end up lowering our standards to feel wanted in some capacity. Our conversation with ourselves becomes the loudest voice we hear. My challenge to you is to know what you deserve and stand up for it, make it more audible.

At the end of the day, courage is another enemy of fear. In your relationships, one person needs to feel inherently loved, and the other person needs to be respected for their pride, the balance of the right and left lobe in the brain. Arguments and disagreements usually come from the imbalance of this. Any dating advice book would tell you this. This can also vary from person to person, and I have experienced both sides of the imbalance. If you truly love the other person, if he gives you things that you know are to both your benefit and not just his own, follow through, be a man, and respect him. In turn, if a man respects you as another, show that you love him and purposely. The heart wants what it wants, and I hope you find yours through the process of letting go and starting again. Breaking up with someone initiates a new beginning.

The Almost Theres

I remember meeting this one guy for a date and not really thinking too much of it. I had just broken up with a guy who was one of the type of guys who didn't get how relationships worked, even though he was nearly ten years older. This guy seemed to have a lot more of his ducks in a row, and it was refreshing, to say the least.

Right off the bat, I knew this guy had a huge heart. A lot of times, clients talk about a certain immeasurable immediate energy being attractive, and his was infectious and so engaging. I think we first connected by being former fat kids. His transition was a bit fresher than mine. I spent years trying to not have any more audible damning self-deprecating internal conversation on my body image. I try to always tell myself that it's how I wear something rather than the actual garments themselves. I think he was still in that transition. The thing about former fat kids is that that conversation seems to never leave; it's how much of the volume you can keep down. Living in Los Angeles gives you a big dose of realism, where you feel like you will always be a swimming manatee in a sea of pretty people, no matter how many carbs you do or don't eat.

Nonetheless, I was not exactly attracted to him physically right off the bat, but I just admired his chivalrous qualities, and that was what grabbed my attention. Was this the one? For me, I always have that moment where I try to see myself being wedded to this person: what it would be like, which Shania Twain song I would dance to on our special day. He seemed to fit this bill, from the surface. We only dated for a short while, but it seemed like one of those relationships where we were not only honeymooning, but it was something that wasn't going to slow down anytime soon. Sometimes I fall hard and quick, but as I get older, I'm a little more cautious and realistic than I used to be.

I remember us getting a little drunk one night, and I thought it was a great idea to bake him a cake. This might have been our very first date; I can't even remember. I do love me some plain yellow cake with sprinkles. After that, he asked if he could kiss me, and we started making out over the steam of our newly baked dessert. I remember him being so open and honest, so vulnerable and trusting. Was that a turn on or what? My admiration now grew to something more physical.

"I simply like you. And I love your eyes. I love that you stood there amongst such a mess of a party, not knowing anyone, but supported me for that crazy little hour last night. I love the way you kiss. I dimly love the way your arms feel near me, wrapped around me, when holding me." This was just a glimmer of the type of radiance this man exposed me to. Every man deserves to feel this way consistently when he is in a loving relationship. Maybe my viewpoint is romantic, but I smile whenever I think about him, and that feeling is enough to convince me.

This guy was in show business and was about to move back east for a job. I found myself getting attached to him so quickly. I mean, if you were texted that, could you not give this a good shot? The thing I have noticed is that I am indeed not a long-distance relationship guy initially, but as I have gotten older, I might be open to it, depending on the communication and how we keep the momentum going. As gay men, we need that element of physicality and proximity in the relationship in the long-term, though. It's hard to have the relationship be glued if the cement seems a little tawdry. I remember lying in bed with him for the last time and knowing that it might be our last time together. I was deeply saddened, but I did feel proud of him that he was going on to bigger and better things.

I remember going to another one of his events with work shortly after we had ended our romantic ties officially, one last hoorah. I remember keeping some of his text messages he sent after our initial departure: "I'm still sitting here a bit shell-shocked, but not a bad thing entirely. I admire you so much. Exactly who you are. Every part of you from the way your eyes move to the way your mouth can curve to your really, really calm/still way about you to the way you leaned back on me at the awards show to your quirky humor that I barely got to witness (or so far, yet). You are a beautiful man, and I appreciate your honesty so, so much. Thank you for blessing me with a really brief glimpse that there's dating that can be had by a man that respectful, passionate, romantic, but also wild and rough and out of the box—just like you did. Thank you, thank you. Have a good night, handsomest."

What an invigorating taste of the true essence of what life is truly about in regard to authentic human experience. The impact of his truth transformed me, even if the entire process didn't give us both the end result we so wished to happen. At the end of the day, the journey to the light at the end of the tunnel was worth every moment I had spent with this man. I never received the light I thought I needed to give me the feeling of completion, but it didn't matter to me. I remember thinking that this was the type of man I would fall in love with one day.

I'm always trying to set up men that don't work out with me with other guys. For some twisted reason, it fulfills me more to know that I can try to make them happy via a trusted third party rather than on my own. I asked him to join one of our singles events, but he quickly took offense and told me he would have trouble with me being there. I think my intentions were good-natured overall, but yes, awkward nonetheless. Doh. He quickly deleted me out of his life abruptly, in every way possible. I guess I cannot blame him. He still liked me, and the wound was still a little fresh. I still slap my hand from this exchange. Sometimes, I need to keep my mouth shut.

Fast-forward to maybe a year later, and I see him out with some friends at a very popular, hipstery gay bar on the eastern side of town. I could tell there was a slight chip on his shoulder, even just based on the way he snidely smiled and looked at me when we engaged in some small talk. He said something along the lines of "Yeah, right" when I told him I would hopefully see him soon. I would have liked to see how he was doing and still be friends, even though I was already exclusively dating someone else at that time. It didn't matter, though. I remembered the impact he gave me in those fonder moments, and that gave me a sense of pride and comfort.

At the end of the day, even with all the bad on how things had ended, I still was so happy that I met this man. When things were good, they were good, and that was enough for my memory bank to grasp. I love how life kind of feels like a bus stop, as one of my married friends noted: there will always be another bus behind the one you just took. This can either go the promiscuous route or the endearing one. I chose the latter. He impacted me in my journey, and I often marvel at how he made me feel. When I meet a suitor that gives me the same warmth he did, I often smile and know that this is worth exploring further.

This story stems from one of the last guys I had met before publishing my book. I felt I was done, but this experience allowed me to close this particular chapter in my life, to write a new work for myself for the future. I felt it needed to be voiced because it taught me so much about myself and how it allowed me to step back and take a view on my life. I really do believe in how the universe presents things to us for a reason.

I remember on one Friday night I had taken one of my girl-friends out to a neighborhood sushi spot for her birthday. One of my more social friends had been trying to get me to hang out with him for months, and every instance he had asked, I was already in bed … at 9:00 p.m. So I mustered up some youthful energy at the age of twenty-eight and made my way downtown after dinner. I had immediately met him at the rooftop at one of those fourteen-dollars-a-glass pretentiously priced wine bars and immediately was greeted by this attractive young man. He and my friend knew each other from back in the day, as they say. I recognized him right away. Because of my insane photographic memory, I remember seeing his profile on a popular dating application and decided to not swipe right because he was visiting from out of the country. He seemed so great on paper with everything else. This happened to be that same guy, who was in the flesh now, with his infectious smile, right in front of me. He had such an active interest in me, and it came from a "He's not from here" in the best way possible. He told me he "wanted to keep the conversation going," or something to that extent, and sat down next to me during his dinner. Our entire group went from outside to inside, and I started to drink wine, while he had an old-fashioned with everyone sitting at the communal dinner table. He was so intriguing to talk to. I couldn't get enough of it. I hid it well, but my attraction to him was electric and riveting. Soon, we hopped to another bar to see another mutual friend of theirs. During our walk, we talked about what we were looking for in a relationship. I told him, and he said he was intimidated by me. This has happened before to me. I mean, we're conversing about kids, me not being a pretentious gay guy, and me being a good person. I told him that a quality I found attractive in men were his friends and how they could say a lot of things about someone's character. How is this intimidating? I have come to find that instead of it being "coming off too strong" label, it's probably a "this guy is more quality so the stakes are higher" type of thing. Trust me, I would be the first person to admit if I was being unreasonable and psycho. Maybe I should just be silent, and then another person I date down the line will tell me I seem too uninterested or he'll simply disappear. I can't win. I remember another friend of theirs commented that we had something special—the kind of hand gesture that pointed to us collectively. We had some more drinks at that bar and then left and headed back to my friend's place where this same guy was staying. To think, the one night I decided to go out was the night I met an amazing guy unexpectedly. How fun and random! We basically did PG-13 stuff that night and fell asleep. Man, was our physical chemistry like a colorful display of fireworks. Some of the best I had experienced. He would consistently tell me that "he wanted me so bad" in the hottest way possible known to man. I had been on this bulking diet and hitting the gym hard at that time, and it was one of the first times someone had told me how perfect my body was. Um, talk about how we all want to look good naked, but it made me speechless, how admired I felt by him, regardless of how imperfect I still felt. I didn't realize how drunk he was until the following day, so maybe that helped with the ignition of the lack of inhibition. That next day, I told him it was refreshing to meet a guy like him. He told me, "Aw, you're the great one. I had fun with you." I immediately thought, *Uh-oh, he only labeled me as "fun."* I really liked him, and he said the same thing, so I was more comforted by that. We had an affinity for country music, we loved shows like Dateline, and we loved staying in and being lazy and watching mindless TV. We had so much in common. I made a joke that we were like Danny and Sandy in *Grease*, and we were in this summer fling that would hopefully last. I was elated. Oh, but Mason, he lives in another country. I had scheduled some social things that weekend, but they all fell through, making me more available to spend more time with him. I felt the universe was pulling for us.

Fast-forward five days, and I basically spent the night with him four out of those five days. We communicated more than once a day when we weren't together. It felt like a natural drug to me, the exchange we had. He had mentioned to his best friend back home that he had met "this amazing guy." He would get jealous of me getting attention from other guys during the Superbowl weekend festivities. He was very vocal about that, because it was "something he was working on." There was this one guy that liked him apparently that someone else invited, and maybe that was him marking his territory, being close to me when he arrived. He would tell me more than once that I could get "any guy I wanted" after I had jokingly said he had a lot of guys waiting for him back in his homeland. He would consistently be flirtatious sexually as well as giving me compliments: "You are so handsome." He would consistently grab me and show me affection almost in a claiming way in front of a sea of gays. It never felt like too much, though. It all felt very, very natural, and I was reciprocating. He would ask if it was okay to hold my hand in public. He was thoughtful and always was the best host. I went with it and was hooked. By the end of that period of time, I actually started looking at flights in the city he had resided and even started looking for a job. I mean, this was for a brief second, but just the thought of having a life with this amazing man, in a different part of the world, sent me into proverbial dreamland. It was for the thrill of adventure, mostly. Yes, I totally take full responsibility for being blinded by the endorphins from my eagerness.

I remember it was the second time we had spent the night together. I remember having a nightmare that woke me with so much anxiety that I couldn't really go back to sleep the rest of the night. He even noticed me not being able to sleep well. I remember being in a plane and knowing that it was about to crash. I then went from the confines of the airline to now the bird's-eye view, where I then witnessed the crash and the flames engulfing both the pilot and copilot from the front of the aircraft. What was my subconscious telling me from this horrific imagery among the fuselage? I think it told me that I was afraid in something I didn't understand. I was afraid of loving someone that I probably couldn't have.

Toward the last of our conversations, I noticed that most of the instigation in conversation had come from me. I had jokingly asked him if he ever initiated conversation. This spiraled into a conversation of "being realistic" and that I shouldn't "get in over my head so fast." Ouch. I was told that what I was saying "was more than just that" and that I "knew this." This just went from 0 to 100. I just told him it shouldn't be so cumbersome to just simply ask how my day was going. He agreed and apologized but seemed severely confused and distraught. But wait, this was my expectation on someone *I was dating*. This may not be someone else's at all or yet. I honestly was getting so many signs that led to me believing that we were heading into something realistic. Maybe I had a point of hopeless romanticism, but I felt shot down real quick. He told me long-distance relationships were hard, and I never had been in one. I told him I was simply excited and that I agreed to a lot of his points, and it's hard to fully know someone in a matter of five or six days. He agreed and wanted to be "slow and cautious." I understood and told him things could be misconstrued via text messages and that this conversation was never meant to have been so heavy. I was quip and ended a lot of points with a smiley face of sorts. I told him he should enjoy his stay in LA, spend time with the people that love him so much, and not have the pressure he thought he was putting himself under by getting to know me. Maybe I was putting too much pressure on him, but I honestly told him I was just listening to the universe and that

I felt we were taking things as they naturally presented themselves. To make sense of things, I remember doing a quick overview of things in my head. I sent him one line that sent him into panicky outer space. Dude, just tell me right there you're not into me like that. I still am bewildered at what I did to make him feel so vehement. He was overwhelmed, and when I told him I was too, he told me I turned things to him that didn't sit well with him. This wasn't about a pursuance issue; it was about miscommunication. Everyone has different ways of dealing with things, and who am I to judge a person I had met practically yesterday. It was not like we were fusing our lives tomorrow; we barely knew each other wholly. I didn't really tell anyone about him, and it was not like we had full-on sex. I thought we were pretty light, considering the whirlwind we had experienced just in one short period. He later told me that I was giving him radio silence after our tiff. He checked on me the next day after the infamous texting string. I did the following, and there I was being blamed for communicating with him differently now. Huh? I'm sorry, I don't keep specific daily tabs on my friends, and I felt I was doing quite well, all things considered. All my close friends are busy, and we are a "start where we left off" type of people. Men I am dating, however, are very different. He did finally say he "never considered us dating." Cool, I'm glad you made that known in black-and-white. If I am correct, he was being realistic about the enjoyment of courting and getting to know me. Um, okay. He seemed to have wanted boyfriend qualities with a person who will accept boyfriend behavior but with no inclination of any process or label. He fused a NSA relationship with an actual one and completely threw me for a loop. Bravo, I can laugh and say I've never heard or experienced that one. Wait, I'm pretty sure I was his trophy for the week. Whatever, this just got too weird to wrap my head around. It seemed a little middle school to me, where we would hold hands in the hallway, present ourselves like love birds (our mutual friend called us), and just talk on the phone or do old-school instant message at night. Luckily, we placed things behind us, and we'll be better friends. I was telling one of my friends after everything that I was usually so much smarter than this, but I guess when we feel our heart beat louder than our mind, we get blinded. Sometimes that works, and sometimes it doesn't. I felt like I went through a whole relationship in a week: from beginning, middle, to end. I was so tired, and I am sure he was too.

I remember walking back to my car after our reunion crew went out for drinks that weekend and started to realize that I did deserve someone special. It was quite the defeating walk because I had to pass local sellers on a grungier part of LA with all the signs of Valentine's Day. Tables with vibrant red roses, lovable teddy bears, and hearts galore adorned the dirtier parts of the corner of Western and Santa Monica Boulevard. Through the grapevine some months later, I was told that he had met someone else during the same time he was visiting, later got engaged to him, parted his time visiting him, and now he is officially moving to America. What I love about this story is that there is so much parallelism here. We both took gambles on things and one time the odds weren't in our favor, and the other time it was victorious for just one party. I could sit here and compare myself to his other choice, laugh at his own inconsistency, or I could look at it as the universe was telling me something, and our separation made him be open to meeting this other, better fit for him. I think putting myself in this position allows me to be happy for him. Because I know that when you experience shades of love, you hold onto and go for it.

That same week, I had met a guy again I had known for a few months briefly through my work events, and he too was also leaving to live in another country. We spent a pleasant Sunday Funday together with an eclectic group of friends. I felt that this was a test. The universe was telling me to maybe make an impact on these two individuals, but maybe it wasn't for us to reach the end result of eventually being in a relationship. Maybe it was for them to change something in me or for me to expose them to something different. I kept that in mind so I wouldn't feel too depressed on things that only happened in a matter of a week's time. Maybe that's my optimism speaking, or that guy could still think I was some lunatic who wanted to marry him tomorrow. It'll be what it'll be. I tried not to get too caught up in it, but all in all, it taught me that I needed to escape LA—I didn't know what that meant. Maybe it was a vacation, or maybe it was to move and feel like I can leave my imprint somewhere else. I'll keep you and myself posted.

I felt like I needed someone who would woo me selfishly and not be intimidated and really love every ounce of who I am initially. Intimidation comes from one person feeling that he's "behind" or "not enough" in some way. I want a guy who feels internally charged by our conversations and also believes it too. At the end of the day, I sat there for a second, and yes, he did live far away, but my heart told me to leap with my arms wide open. I could have fallen, or I could have flown. I never would have known if I didn't try. We spend a lot of our lives testing people, and sometimes we just need to fall and feel like an idiot. The good thing about falling is that we always learn from it, can laugh at ourselves, and usually dust ourselves off easily. This might be very wishful thinking, but what if he was the soul mate that came into my life with so much coincidental circumstance, and I just let it be unnoticed as something that could have been extraordinary? It's so funny; I remember interviewing someone that same day just hours after our conversation, mentioned prior. The person I had been interviewing had dated someone from that same city, and the distance wasn't even the main issue to that relationship's demise. This entire experience taught me about that initial electric spark. I remember him coming into my apartment and remember shocking him a couple of times when I leaned in to kiss him. Friction and scientific assumption aside, it was just a reminder of how fulfilled I was, and it made me realize that I deserve this feeling. I found that over the years, some of my more successful matches had this right away. It was a simply put "I felt a spark, and we really like each other." There's distinctive power in it. It also taught me to go with my gut. I liked this guy, and it felt so natural on both ends, I believe, to spend time together consecutively and to feel like we were creating something special despite a prominent geographic obstacle. It wasn't like I hadn't been in a relationship before and was all googly-eyed by the thought of a boy liking me. He made me feel safe, or maybe I didn't know yet what it was, but I was okay with it being unidentified and mysterious.

I didn't need the validation of being in a committed relation-ship with this person. I felt I had validated my feelings for me, and that was enough. That was my truth, and for that, I am proud I got to experience it through my mind, body, and spirit. It's something I will always treasure and remember for the rest of my life.

What's Your Love Language?

Gary Chapman's, *The 5 Love Languages®*, is a resource I enjoyed reading in the past. I would implore any existing relationship to read this book to make it stronger. His theory looks at how each person communicates love to one another: a language. Dr. Chapman breaks it down to five types of love: Quality Time, Acts of Service, Receiving Gifts, Physical Touch, and Words of Affirmation. Being your own love detective is how I see this working and strengthening a relationship between you and your significant other.

Let me personally break this down for you. I am a tie between Acts of Service and Quality Time. I hover over the Words of Affirmation category too. Therefore, the more my significant other understands my love language, the better our relationship will be in the long-term. My significant other can touch me all he wants, but if he is "physical touch", he is fulfilled, but here I am, feeling empty and unloved. Keep in mind, how you interpret "I love you" can be very different from your counterpart. A selfless way of thinking can make you and your potential become selfishly closer in the progression to something more solid over time. I have seen many accounts on how one partner rewires their understanding of their partner's love language, and it completely renovated and renewed their relationship as a whole.

This ideal also comes down to knowing that your expectation of dating is not everyone else's ledger. I would get so let down when a guy wouldn't text me right away, within an hour. The main reason why I have more of a sense of urgency is that my "Words of Affirmation" quality is a bit louder, while everything else can be a bit more muted in this concept. I need someone who will let me know what he wants to do with me ahead of time. Nothing is sexier than having a man take initiative and take time out of his chaotic life to plan things to do with me in advance. "Wear your favorite suit, and I'll pick you up at six p.m. for dinner on Friday. I got the rest." If someone said that to me every once in a while, you might as well slurp me through a straw off the floor. I also love doing that in return for someone. I think, for me, it's to create conversations of balance and gratitude. You know, having your loved one realize that you have a certain way about things, and him reciprocating by listening to you and actually fulfilling the request. It's important to show gratitude when someone else shows change for the better of the relationship. Please mind your p's and q's, and chivalry certainly isn't dead; people just choose not to do it. Don't be lazy. It's positive reinforcement 101, duh. You give the dog a treat after he sits, he keeps doing it, right?

It's important to identify this understanding as a form of a symbiotic relationship. You know, two unexpected parts that might be quite different on their own, but create this retrospective conglomerate effort over time. It's important to look at love languages like this, as an enhancing, nondescriptive communication style between couples. Some people don't even realize their type of communication until it's laid out in front of them. For me, I didn't even realize that I find so much joy in planning events together and doing things like washing dishes and preparing meals when my significant other has had a long day. Some men see that as me doing those things for them, but honestly, it fills my soul to do those things without even a prompt. At the end of the day, I at least wish to receive a form of gratitude for me sharing my communication style to them.

Ever have one of those working relationships where everything literally clicks seamlessly? Not only are you on the same wavelength anatomically, but you also probably share some of the same love languages. Appreciation is a facet of love. The more you feel appreciated, the better your relationship will be with someone, barring the environment and context of the relationship. I've set people up in the past where the feedback was nominal but straightforward. "Mason, we had a great first date. We just get each other." Sometimes we are our own worst enemies. We convolute things by making assumptions, which can impede our attractions. Another client was so adamant about "men being too busy to date him," when all he did was read their profile. We shouldn't jump the gun until we are presented factual evidence through experiences that give us patterns. I do a little sleuthing on how their dating expertise works or fails them based on similar patterns in feedback from different people. Okay, so he's rescheduled the date twice and doesn't bother to initiate conversation; okay, different story, buddy. Sometimes being you is enough, and sometimes that "enough" is someone else's "enough." Love is something that sometimes seems like a secret. When you date someone, you might feel like things are naturally just there. My theory is that certain personality traits and upbringing usually yield similar love language patterns. For instance, a man who is obsessed with physical fitness usually yields more into the realm of Physical Touch. A man who is constantly in the confines of a schedule loves Quality Time and constant, effortless communication—Words of Affirmation. When I apply my theory to my own life, I definitely see a definitive correlation here. I grew up around very generous mentors my entire life, which adds to my affinity toward Acts of Service to the assessment altogether. One of the best ways a boyfriend once told me he liked me was, who barely had any expendable money, I might add, threw a dinner together made from his microwave, some red wine in a red Solo cup, with a handwritten note. He could barely make a piece of toast. It was the fact that he took time to really be methodical in a very selfless, caring way that really allowed my attraction to him to grow. He was speaking my Quality Time and Acts of Service love language proficiently.

It's all about communication, chemistry, and compatibility. You have to have all three, and these things hover into most of the qualities mentioned prior. I find that a lot of matchmakers and relationship coaches do advocate for this universal mantra-like equation. You have to have all three. If you have communication and chemistry but no compatibility, you are walking into friends-with-benefits territory; no chemistry, but everything else, you might have just met your best friend. Sometimes chemistry and compatibility are things you can't change, but how you communicate can make the other variables escalate if you are being intelligent about being aware of your potential's best receptive language. I will say, communication is responsible for the perpetuation of the relationship. If you haven't noticed already, I stress that a lot. I feel also Words of Affirmation yields itself to be popular in the gay community. We gays don't like to communicate in retrospect, and when we do, sometimes it's with a dirty sock in our mouths. And well, Physical Touch is up there with us too, for obvious reasons.

Online Dating Treachery

"Some people complain about all of my photos being shirtless, but I'll include one when I find one"—person's dating profile on a popular dating application. Yes, that was all of it. "I brought a knife with me just in case you wanted to steal my kidney"—a girlfriend's real testimony on a first date from a popular dating application. "I don't drink coffee, but I flirt with the baristas at Starbucks for free stuff, then give it away. It's a power thing. Okay, so are you turned off yet? Where in L.A. do you live?"—someone giving me their best first impression on a very popular dating website. This, my friends, are the people out there of our generation. Faceplant.

I remember one year I was so ready to get back out in the dating world. I had reinstalled a couple of popular dating applications and reactivated my profile on a popular dating site. I made a conscious effort to make a great first impression. I was ready! If we matched, or the other party showed interest, I was the first to start the conversation. I remember writing in one of those applications, "You are probably not into me if you take more than 2 or 3 days to start or continue a conversation. Can I get an Amen?" I stuck to that mentality. At one point, I had started a conversation with probably a dozen different guys. I cannot tell you how many of these men, to my detriment, flaked on the date, didn't even respond, completely disappeared, or misrepresented themselves in what they are looking for in regard to a significant other. This is one of the main reasons why I would talk to and keep it pretty casual with multiple people at once: I knew a majority would mostly likely fail, speaking merely in statistical evidence and not pessimism. Sure, everyone loves options, but bad options don't even count or just go unnoticed. I kinda saw this type of dating like a controller of a soundboard. There are so many knobs in front of you, which will turn up slightly when a good date or conversation happens with each one. It's the person that actually goes the extra mile that makes that one knob produce that sound which emerges from background noise to predominant sound, and everything else sorta fades out. There's an increase in volume when there is an increase in apparent propulsion. All in all, we have evolved as a gay species from a social feline with an inquisitive nature to a millennial, torpid sloth. My favorite was when I would write something and someone would respond with a "cool" or a "sounds nice." What. The. Hell. No wonder all the gays hate online dating. You do all this best-foot-forward stuff with very little to no reward at all. Our boredom turns into frustration and disappointment at lightning speed.

My theory is that because these types of avenues are a complementary service or for something very nominal, the less people care in regard to respect and accountability. The less something costs, the less accountability you have. Because I was working in a matchmaking service with people paying a membership fee, it's just a different ball game. You pay your rent because it's a priority. You go to a drive-through because you are broke or want something quick. Each of those examples has value of some kind. Imagine if we went to a restaurant that gave out cheeseburgers for free all the time. I bet you the restaurant itself over time would become a pigsty, the meat would be overcooked or underdone, the customer service would be atrocious, and people would take advantage of it. All those things are bad. You get what you pay for. A lot of people look at any dating platform as a tool where you "have nothing to lose"; however, people that let you down or you let them down, sometimes unintentionally, feel like they have lost something. This something could be time, money, or just emotional energy. I totally understand why some people take long sabbaticals from online or mobile dating in general and letting the universe take the reins.

Remember back in the day when you would tell people, "I'll call you when I get home?" That seems like decades ago, but in fact, it's almost like yesterday speaking from a historian's point of view. The millennial generation has a lot of nerve. Wow, our attention span is now less than one second just from a simple swipe or tap on our phone. I remember reading an enlightening statistic about a very popular dating application. If you placed all the men you have went through, including the duds and thumbs-up, you would only mutually match with about 1.6 percent of them. You then will only meet around 0.8 percent of them in person. Let's not even take into account if there will be initial chemistry in person. I get it. It's so frustrating to feel like you are writing one hundred letters, less than two read it, and you might get one response. When I mentioned this to a friend of mine, he said, "I feel I would have better chances at Powerball." Um, yes, you would.

This became really apparent to me when I was trying to set up a first date with a younger Australian man. I offered to meet him for a coffee or drink. He was severely perplexed and asked why we couldn't just get to know each other over dinner. When I told him, "Welcome to LA and America, where things are fast, cheap, and impersonal." I was refreshed that he implored that request because I like the traditional nostalgia that stemmed from it. I almost felt like he was one of those little kids that looked at me like I was a cool kid, and he was asking me if he could be on my team. I had sent him a photo of my friends and I out the previous night, and he immediately said something along the lines of if I would be disappointed if he wasn't as fit as he appeared to be. He was on this tangent of not being looked at by other men because he didn't have a ripped, hard stomach and a big dick. I'm like, we have to have physical attraction, yes, but sex is on the lower end of the totem pole for me. It was terrible to see that being in LA polluted his confidence and so quickly. On the other end, I see so many transplants from their small town in Oklahoma who are so wholesome and then become a pretentious brat when they come to a major metropolitan city like LA. I often wonder why this permeation is so easy for a lot of individuals. Overall, I feel like East Coasters and Europeans have this style and of being straightforward, but oh, we West Coasters are just swipe-swiping away with our heads in the free-floating clouds.

I recently saw something on TV that allowed me to take a dramatic pause in regard to the date practice of our current generation. I believe it was on a major news channel like CNN, which basically recounted a present-day prom, where no one at the table spoke across it but through their phones instead. In this day, we are surrounded by convenience. A lot of semicasual chain restaurants are receiving a huge decline in business because more convenient and cheaper fast-food chains are outnumbering them. Think about why. Taking the easy way out is sure to allow you to be like every other gay man in a city of beautiful people. This is the nature of our beast in meeting people nowadays. Le sigh.

When I date online, there's most of everything in front of me, which I like. I see compatibility as having two glasses side-by-side, one empty and the other full to the brim. I'll add and subtract water from one glass to the other. It's mostly about checks and balances with me. When the glass feels half-empty, it's definitely a no-go on my end; when it's half-full, what's a coffee date and an hour of my time? For me, I don't have too many requirements. I'll date shorter men, but if they are successful entrepreneurs. I will not date someone shorter who is a person trying to figure their life out. I'm more forgiving with looks if a guy is older than his early thirties. And by that, my expectation is not to date a model—they never want to eat ice cream anyway. I am not attracted to men who are gargantuan in muscular build and with tattoos. However, I am more inclined to date someone with tattoos and that are also leaner in build. Too many tattoos, regardless of age, aren't attractive to me. I don't do well with men in a romantic sense who are creative types. I found I am more attracted to men who are more composed in nature and not extremists. I can't date someone who ejaculates and eats his own semen because a yoga mentor told him it was good for his internal process and is "good for him." I wish I was kidding with you. So you can kind of see how I can fill the glass then take some away, but sometimes the glass spills, and all you can do is giggle and leave it be. I'd like to think through all these experiences, I have taken a piece of them and started to create a mosaic of what I think I need and deserve.

This metaphor also can be applied to actually setting up the first meeting. If I've been trying to tip my glass to your favor to meet you, I am running on empty and out of patience. I am way too old and intelligent for a pen pal. One of my dear friends in LA met "the love of his life" via mutual friends. What was so special was that this guy that was pursuing him was a little wishy-washy in the beginning. However, my friend finally said that if he wished to meet him for a drink, it would have to be at this time and in this area because he was going to be going out of town for an extended amount of time. The gentlemen obliged and went out of his way to be in hours of traffic, to spend just an hour with him. Swoon central, and this act blew my friend out of the water. This man found the convenient in the inconvenient. He went out of his way to prove that the other person was worth his time. That, my dear friends, is the best way to make someone feel like they matter.

I had a client one time asking me why dating was sounding like a script to him. To be frank, it's hard not to. Sometimes you have to ask dynamic, open-ended questions. Instead of asking someone, "What do you do?" you should phrase it this way, "Why do you do what you do," or "What inspired you to take your career path?" Notice one angle is very logistic, and the other allows you to peek inside of someone's personality. Doing this allows you to feel personal internal compatibility, which is the source of a budding anatomic physiological attraction, in my humble opinion. Some of those "Let things happen naturally/organically" people are also ones to get offended if they feel like they are being tested. Newsflash, dating will and always be a test. Not necessarily something with a bullet-point-oriented agenda, but it's still some sort of test. I tried five boxes of a specific brand of cereal before I settled with the right one. It's consistent, nourishing, fulfilling, and gives me the same joy every time, without fail. Therefore, we're in a relationship of some sorts, and it's a delicious one at that.

The studies from Coffee Meets Bagel, a dating application I was researching, had that distinctive affinity as well. It's not about how I feel about your dating profile; it's about the fifty other people that online-date like you and have similar outcomes, whether that be good or bad. It's elementary, dear Watson, in the measurable amounts of quantitative and qualitative data. We now enter the world of adulting. Although we praise ourselves about doing things on our own like making a grilled cheese sandwich, we actually don't yield behaviors that support that inclination in date practice. I mean, why wash your own car or clothes when someone else can easily come and do it for you with the click of a button? The convenience is a saturation of hindrance to our own character. We get so used to having things done for us from another party, rather than on our own time and dime. The permeation dilutes the responsibility we give ourselves.

"Initially, I thought single people must be lazy.

They don't bother to put anything interesting on their profile, and then go off complaining on how online dating sucks. Why don't you write more on your profile? Why won't you say something more than 'Hi?'" This is an account from the CEO that said these indolent daters "are not doing this because they are lazy, but because they are afraid. See, if they really put thoughts and efforts into writing something that describes themselves, and they don't get liked back, or if they try to have real conversations and don't hear back, that's a real rejection. So, instead, they pretend not to care, to choose not to open up so much."

What is interesting about this is that, even with the emotional standpoint, which can be fairly unpredictable and ambiguous, there is still a measurable portion of solid data here. Therefore, what the CEO found was that, without being vulnerable or caring, you are just hindering your own dating experience and increasing your detriment of singleness. It can almost be determined that giving more energy and being rejected is better than not giving enough and continuing to be rejected. Call me an optimist, but I am always in favor of trying my best, and knowing that is good enough for me. Be proud of yourself for taking the leap and going through your own journey to your own destination.

People ask me all the time about my honest opinion on mobile dating applications. I honestly feel you use them how you want and shouldn't judge others by how you or they do it. Think of it this way, in the 1950s, date practice was very traditional and chivalrous, and then the infusion of technology and impersonal date practices polluted our opportunities of true engagement. Now it's so easy to find partnered men searching for other men on these avenues, which I think has made it so convenient to stray away from the traditional viewpoint of yesteryear. It's such a cat-and-mouse game. We need to follow more of the "Yes and..." improvisation rule, where we perpetuate a conversation as opposed to ending it.

He asks how my day is going, and I respond in one word. He tells me hi, and I ignore it. He says hello, and I might respond. He greets, asks how my day is going, and I send a more racy photo or a photo that is me but is probably just my facial profile. He then responds with "Handsome" or "Cute" and tells me he is either going or coming from the gym. Verbal flattery is amateur in this sense, of looking through a sea of headless svelte torsos. I get it; it's the least amount of effort, because being on dating applications isn't really where you meet the love of your life, most likely. However, expect the least amount of effort back. The unimaginative monotony makes me want to inflict pain on myself. I mean, if I chat with twenty guys, I may wind up meeting one. What a bad statistic and a lot of frustration in the hopes of finding a normal person in the sea of anus, penis, and an occasional sex toy if I'm trying for "No Whammy." I get it, though; Some people don't get a response because they are too far out of the parameters of what you are looking for maybe in age, ethnicity, or geographic location. Yes, most of these things are logistic, but it's not like you would approach these people at a bar in person if they were twenty years your senior or visiting from four thousand miles away in Norway. You have to find the fairness in the ambiance and flow of these avenues. My patience boiling point is usually lukewarm. I don't give people the benefit of this doubt as much, and I unmatch or dismiss people all the time if I have reached out and haven't gotten a response, or the responses are days apart from one another. Maybe I am just too literal and results-oriented for my own good. The reason I do that, though, is having too much low dangling fruit gives me too much frustration, so I just toss it out; it doesn't serve me in a positive way. We get frustrated with good starts that end in horrific or unsatisfied endings. Dating applications in general are a game changer for the millennial generation and people who date actively in it, despite their own age. Success comes in all forms, shapes, and sizes. The thing about these avenues is that it's the act of infection of frustration that can seem to never go away, but we'll come back to them again and again. I usually go in spurts. I'll be on them for a couple of weeks, I'll meet someone and then date them, and then I might start again. Sometimes I need a break from them. I guess I am just a really good filter with whom I open my time. I have never been on them for the sole purpose of hooking up. Okay, maybe two or three times if I am being honest. I usually did that when I was younger and met those guys at bars on my own. To be candid, I'd rather just jack off, and then I don't have the urge anymore to have sex with anything with an orifice. You'll feel better doing the deed with someone whom you actually like, and that's enough reward for me to be patient. I would get so mad about differing timelines in dating when using these applications. I found it so offensive that men who did want a relationship, who promised a coffee, would cease and desist anything, even though I would see them active on the same application every single day. I need to meet you, for goodness sake. I don't want to get to know you via text of sorts. We gay men sometimes like to have all these options, and sometimes really good ones at that, but we actually never follow through with them. It's kind of like us being able to go to the grocery store for free, picking out everything we want and never making it to the checkout stand, but we'll continue to go back for yet another variety of hummus. Huh? I'm confused. Talk about rapacious, indeed. I never got that mentality, and I found it more annoying than rewarding. In turn, sometimes I was overwhelmed and would get hit up constantly, and some of those matches would sit because I would be more inclined to strike up conversation with them if they showed more interest in the beginning. Some guys, though, who seemed more initially compatible, I would always reach out to them first. I treated everyone as individuals, though, and went with my head rather than my heart in these instances. If a man was genuine and wrote something eloquent, even if the match wasn't there, I would try to make an effort to at least respond, show gratitude, but be honest. When using these avenues, expect someone to completely disappear, even after there was conversation that seemed so optimistic and real. Expect a person to maybe flake. For me, I expect someone to always disappear midconversation so I won't get my hopes up, but I can sometimes be a harsh realist. Expect a person to surprise you too, in a good way. It's a huge gamble.

One of my favorite dating application stories was an account of a guy going ballistic on another because he was eating something with nuts in it, and the other guy seemed to be severely anaphylactic-shock-allergic to nuts. So when guy 1 was going to give the other a proverbial mouth hug, the other guy I guess thought the other was about to murder him. "It was like an innocent dinner and a movie, no talk of any sex, and he went from 0 to 100. That's gay life. He needs your book."

I recommend people to use dating apps if sexual compatibility is at the top of their list. It's full sexual transparency. However, this guy might not have a career, might be into drugs, be an illegal immigrant, or be dishonest in general, who knows! I remember receiving an e-mail that told me about this man having a "huge, gigantic dick" and that he wished to meet a "professional, well-educated, pliant man." You could tell that this guy was a highly sexual person, saying he loved "clothing-optional beaches to relax" as one of his interesting fact icebreakers for one of our singles events. He sent his inquiry from a very genuine standpoint, even sending me another e-mail the next day telling me that and apologizing if he offended me. He told me he had been in a marriage for over a decade, and his partner could never really take it. He told me he could get all these men to "play with it," but it seemed some other pieces were missing in that process. He had been trying for four years thus far to find his ideal match of the mental and the obvious physical. "It was simply too big to deal with and certainly not in a relationship [for those men I was trying to date]—it's a blessing and a curse." Therefore, he, along with everyone else like him, would use dating applications as a sieve for optimal sexual pleasure and experience. With that, you actually engage in sexual acts and can be thrown to the side like a piece of trash, or you might actually be dealing with one too, once everything is said and done. So ask yourself, is sex *that* important to you? Good luck.

So both of you are down to meet each other. You made it through the obstacle course, blindfolded, but you are finally here. Hooray. Mind you, you might not know much about this person, or you might have been chatting away before the initial meet. Professionally, I've always told people to not reveal as much beforehand, and to not take offense to men who don't check in multiple times even if they'd solidified their initial meet way in advance. Sometimes, unfortunately, it might seem like a business meeting before you meet, but it shouldn't feel like that in person. I always recommend going the casual route. Go out for happy hour, lunch, a coffee, or my favorite, a brunch date. If coffee is the better bet for scheduling, go for a cozy café feel, and be careful the date doesn't seem too "businessy." The check comes, okay, who pays? If you ask someone for a more formal date, you pay. It's the gentlemanly thing to do. If you cancel the first date, you pay for the rescheduled one. It's also the gentlemanly thing to do. Plus, if you like him enough, pay for the first time, and he can pay for the next one. It's like your secret insurance policy of interest. If you are keeping things really casual, you both just pay on your own. No need to place a label on something if from the beginning you both seem of equal and even interest. With dates in general, I love to schedule around midday because an individual isn't tempted to get sloppy, and the person is able to sleep in, probably to get a work out in, it's an hour of their time, and if they cancel you, you still have the whole day unplanned ahead of you. Trust me, you'll know after a half hour, if there is a second date in the future. Going casual gives you an easy out, just in case the initial meeting is a total dud. Dinner dates can very much be a gamble. I get it, though; some men are more traditional and old-school, and they want to be a chivalrous gentleman. But oh my gosh, let's say the chemistry isn't there, and you are only through the appetizers. No one wants to see you claw the table and be anxious to leap out the window. It always feel nice to ask or to be asked on a dinner date anyway. It's nostalgic quality. Be a man, and tell the other guy where to go and what time. I can remember so many times where a guy said, "I am around this weekend, but don't know my plans yet." Okay, fair enough, but he said that on a Monday. It is now Friday afternoon. You are just not that into me if you are playing this "If something better pops up" scenario. If you meet and there's no chemistry, just be honest and say "I enjoyed getting to know you, but I just don't feel the physical chemistry," or

"I enjoyed our date, but feel we are not as compatible as I wished." If you don't feel comfortable doing it in person, as I do at times, send a simple text, and be cordial. You do this because it's the adult thing to do, thank you very much.

I remember going out one night in the LA gay scene and remember feeling so angered by what I was witnessing. What I wish could happen was for everybody to drop their phones at the door and get to know one another. As much as I preach to get out there to experience human interaction, even at this overcapacity dance club, people where still swipe-swiping and tick-tacking on the dance floor, laughing with their friends about who they would choose. Even the guy dancing on a platform near his private table was shaking his booty while choreographing his hand motion in his routine of picking his suitor, while there was the white glare on his face from his cell phone. My friend and I made the comment that everyone there looked like they could be on some CW show. So even in social situations, with all this eye candy in front of them, they still are still glued to instant gratification. Oh, how I wish times were how they were back in the olden days. It's disappointing that the start of mobile and Internet dating has caused such a rift in the classic way of communication. It's almost like we feel safer hiding behind a persona than being who we are as a human. People like to hide and can make themselves appear better in a profile photo that took them thirty minutes to perfect through some strategic filtering.

How you date as a person usually has some correlation in your verbiage in your online dating profiles. I'm sure you are more interesting than "music, food, and traveling." I'm sure you have more hobbies than "stuff." My favorite is a person's bio saying he's "low-key" and "seeing what's out there." I've mentioned this before, so you should take a big hint. Um, big next. It's all about allowing the other person to see inside your personality. "I am a big foodie and want someone who will cry with me when I emotionally eat my Ben & Jerry's." Just that one statement shows an adventurous nature, a go-with-the-flow attitude, with some playful humor. It's almost about decoding the first impression code. Another pet peeve of mine is someone who has "no expectations" or someone who is "not taking life too seriously."

Your coy attitude is annoying. Period. Sure, everyone wants to date a person with an easygoing and adventurous personality. Duh. No one wants to date someone dull. I've been wondering for years what the hell that means because I probably see that in profiles 60 percent of the time, if not more. Maybe this is more of verbiage I would see in major metropolitan cities as well as I create this correlation. I'm pretty sure no one is putting "anal retentive" and "narrow-minded" in the qualities they are looking for in their profiles. I've narrowed it down to gay men feeling like they need an easier out both emotionally and physically. Nowadays, gay men want to be perceived as having options. Some men also are very simple people, but in the sea of gregarious personalities in LA, men want to meet dynamic men with a prism of interests right from the get-go. I also find that this is a big slippery slope. So since you are so easygoing about dating, you must be okay with someone not confirming a date the day before or maybe even canceling at the eleventh hour. Last time I checked, "easygoing" people are kind of roll-with-the-punches types. Having expectations is extremely attractive to people along the same mind-set. Knowing what you want and being vocal about it is an attribute that can either be intimidating or attractive to someone. Other guys will just label you as "too much" because they just aren't where you are at, and that's an admirable quality. As a disclaimer, if you are over thirty, you ought to have some expectations. However you define that in this point in your life, you should care how you spend your time dating and with whom. Be your own filter in your profile. You should "be too much" and let the other floozies deter themselves from you to save you the wasted energy. Over the years, I find that a lot of men have told me that I seem really genuine and straightforward based on my wording that I had written in my online dating profile. Those same men and I would most likely meet for a date. By no means do I feel like I am some famous orator. I was just honest and used good punctuation and grammar. When asking another matchmaker at our office about some memorable profile moments, one of the people who applied to be in our database eloquently wrote, "I'm blonde, tan, and pretty." I'll leave that there for you to digest on your own.

Yes, pictures are awkward, but that is just the way the cookie crumbles. I cannot tell you how many men say "I don't take too many pictures." Um, really. I seriously doubt that. Maybe it's more accurate to say, "I feel I am unphotogenic and avoid photos altogether." I am a big stickler for good ones. I'm not talking about the whole photo shoot enchilada. Please don't pretend to be a model. Nothing is more awkward than somebody pretending to be someone they're not. Please don't place your hand on your hips, choke your tie, or place your hands on your thumbs through your belt loop. Calm down, cowboy. Any intuitive human can look at your photo for five seconds and know something is off. As a matchmaker, my job is to facilitate the best first impression I can possibly do for you. Since we all know gay men are the worst at quick judgments on the visual scale, I have a lot to lose on sole mediocrity. Don't be so judgmental either. I need just enough attraction to want a date with you, about 60 percent. Anything less than that is dead on arrival, unfortunately. I have found over the years that the best photos that one can use to get more yeses are not selfies. Selfies can give a pretentious vibe, and a man wants to see your body type before he makes an investment in taking two more additional seconds to scan your other photos or maybe make the trek to scroll down and read your bio. Oh, pursed duck lips and interrogative expressions, you unamaze me. I don't care to see your shirtless bathroom selfie. I'm staring at your dirty toilet anyway, which it seem like you never clean. I will say some guys do take good selfies, but it's is very hard to balance looking natural in something that can be seen as narcissistic, contrived, and strange. Eyes are the windows to the soul and good for energy reading; sunglasses block this. I don't care to see your cap on your head unless it is a stylish fedora. Don't be ashamed if you are balding or don't have enough hair. Bald men can be very sexy. Are you obsessed with your nephew? It seems so since he's in every picture. Wait, is he your child? I love the fact that you are in a group of your hot friends. Too bad I find your friend more attractive than you. I love that you went to Paris, but the Eiffel Tower is distracting me from you. Being *you* in your own natural environment shows you being confident. You are just fine just the way you are, promise. Men are attracted to more masculine parts of your body, which are your shoulders, chest, and arms. Think about why baboons beat their chests in the wild. It's a representation of power and confidence that we were taught even as youngsters playing that role. If you were taking a few notes, these photos, my friends, are your winners.

Most people desire to be in love in some sense, but sometimes they are the most guilty playing this role at their own frustration. I always like to know I am working toward something. If I just wanted to chat with strangers, I would do so on my own accord, and not on a dating website, which is meant for dating. Having your friends set you up, to me, is the best way to get dates, and even if they're bad, you can laugh about it—you only live once. I'd rather the referral come from a friend than playing the dice roll with a complete stranger. This isn't rocket science.

Wired for Love

You start to get excited when you see someone you deem attractive. Your pupils dilate, and your nervous system responds because of the stimulation from serotonin that is released in your body. Your heart rate and blood pressure might escalate to your physical awareness. Your adrenaline increases, and you start to maybe get aroused both mentally and physically. Norepinephrine is released during stimulation, making certain areas of your body feel more sensitive or maybe lighter. Other stimuli induce dopamine and oxytocin, which are our happy chemicals, which give a sense of elation. This, my friends, is the anatomical response of attraction. Our sense of smell has been said to be our most memorable sense, and we sometimes revert back to connections that felt so good to our souls in our pasts, and that reminder allows attraction to develop as well. Pheromones are an ardent physiological response that draws us to someone we are attracted to. Ever have one of those guys you could just smell all day? Well, there you go. Your body was meant to feel the pleasure of relationships. Think of it as long-term, though, rather than a continuous cycle of multiple encounters that seems more regular. This process is addicting. In my opinion, doing it too often with different people hinders your body from building a true connection.

It amazes me how all of us are wired a certain way, no matter our gender or sexual orientation. Take an inventory of how you are in your work environment and what your contributions are within it. This inventory is a great gauge to identify your side. Also, there are many theories of how this develops based on how you were raised as a child. Highly logical and analytical types are left brained (LB). LB men are usually punctual, detail oriented, and extremely organized. These guys are usually lawyers, software developers, doctors, accountants, and politicians. More creative types would be right brained

(RB). These guys would identify themselves as artists and usually are in some kind of creative field. RB men are big-picture people and usually find their form of Zen in chaotic environments. It's the guy whose place is a disaster, but can find everything buried under piles of random stuff.

The premise I see about this issue comes from planners versus nonplanners, especially in the study of individuals living in more metropolitan cities. I looked at my dating résumé in its entirety, and I noticed that I have the LB mentality down to a science. I also noticed that I have met men who are more LB than me, making me switch to more of the spontaneous RB one. I do see shifts from time to time. You have to look within yourself and see if that imbalance is tolerable. Other men define it as a necessity. To each his own. I was just having a chat over coffee with one of my gorgeous girlfriends, and I swear we are the same person. My mother would be ecstatic to have me marry her. Too bad we don't play for the same team. We are the type of people to sit down and plan our weekends out sometimes a month in advance. I feel valued from initiation and the fusion of someone making the time to make themselves available for me. I am an expert at making time for someone in return, even when I have a zillion things on my plate. There just has to be a mutual progression and give and take before I give myself permission to go into this process of giving my time to someone. Time is our most valuable resource as humans. RB men who are more go with the flow are either intimidated by how much we can fit in our day sanely as LB individuals, or it isn't for them, and they jump ship. Let them freely swim to the horizon, find their "spiritual awakening," while we both build two more ships by the time they find their way back to us.

It's actually no different than straight relationships in brain pattern attraction. We are just a shell, and everything is different on the inside, our wiring. Once I started realizing that a man's physical body is merely a vessel for his heart and soul, it allowed me to see the insight of the interior before I started noticing the perceptible exterior. I was then able to say to myself, "Yes, he's attractive, but now what?" I also say this especially in how I am as a businessman. Everyone has dated the model, had their fun, and then got bored, so here I am being hired as their matchmaker. Looks are only so much, believe me. In this model, age is honestly just a number; a young man sat across my desk and reminded me of a more attractive version of Morgan Freeman. He dogmatically told me that dating men over forty-five caused him to turn gray prematurely. They seemed so wishy-washy to him, not knowing what they wanted, and I could argue that I have met a lot more men in their twenties with the same type of ambiguous behavior. I have met men who are in their late twenties and already have a house, savings, and the whole shebang. In turn, I've met men who are in their midforties still apartment living, a professional bartender, and who have accepted the stigma and responsibility of that lifestyle. It's easy for us to say, "He's thirty-five, and he *should* have these things together." Sometimes, my friends, he doesn't, at all. That's why it's important to see things from the inside first. Do be careful of generational differences, though. Sometimes when someone is referring to the Spice Girls, it can be a little awkward when one is reminiscing of his Three Dog Night days. Age can be just a number, but there is a logical assessment to that, as mentioned prior. Also, you want someone who can probably naturally meld with the majority your friends, who are most likely around 5 to 10 years of your own age. I have seen men who wouldn't normally date each other because of age, because they date the same younger men. Great minds think alike, yes? One of my favorite clients was whisked away like a teenage schoolboy by someone slightly older than him when he would prefer to date someone ten or more years younger. Knowing both of them, they loved that same cookie-cutter boy with that same frosting and other adornments. I love seeing something unexpected work to everyone's best advantage. Randomly, I have heard multiple older men tell me they prefer to date a "man with a car." Seems like someone was getting tired of being someone's chauffeur and dating younger, not-as-settled men who were taking the bus in one of the busiest and most traffic-heavy city in the country. Regardless, I want to work or date someone with a clear path of what they desire and need from someone, their value of the interior, which can reflect the visible exterior. This usually comes with a car, in this sense. It's like some people are on a continuous loop in a regular car, and then others are in monster trucks that veer from time to time on that same path. This is a huge part of initial frustration when trying to get to know someone. Our terrains can all be very different. At the end of the day, I get that we are a gay community that has this impenetrable search for the fountain of youth. Sometimes younger guys who date older, turn into older guys who date younger. There has to be a very sharp correlation in the paths of both parties, given many generational differences and some behavioral brain patterns. You have to ask, is that generation gap going to enhance the inquisitive nature of the relationship or cause too many unsuitable differences?

I met this charming older lesbian couple at an event one time, and they have been together for almost thirty years. I had asked why they liked each other. One of the women barely mentioned the other's looks, but stressed other admirable qualities, like sense of humor and kindness. When I'm meeting people, I start from the inside out, and that naturally allows the exterior to become more attractive over time. Who doesn't like instant gratification? But patience gives a sense of respect for the individual. We start with physical chemistry, but emotional chemistry is really what gets our juices flowing. The intellectual stimulation hits our core. I remember at one point in my life when I was consistently being bribed to go on dates with celebrities or men of prestige and power. I honestly didn't give a shit. Your undercover conversation to your friend I overheard about hookers and blow does not make me want to introduce them to my mother, ever, in this lifetime. At the end of the day, are you even going to make time for me anyway? Big "*Next.*"

I had met a young straight couple at a birthday event where the man was definitely the girl in the relationship, and the girl was the guy. This man was well dressed and an entrepreneur of a prestigious distribution company. The young lady had a tough skin, almost intimidating. They complemented each other so well and were actually engaged at that time. Put presumed gender roles and sexuality behind you for a second. In my opinion, RB men make great fathers; they are usually the culprits of spoiling their female children into Daddy's girls. I'm not emasculating anyone; I'm merely presenting facts. Once you see it as that, there is a huge decrease in offense.

Seeing my parents be married for thirty-six years gave me also a great example of relation. My father being the RB and my mother being the LB. My dad was always the type to run away from structure and loved working at his own pace and at the beat of his own creative drum. My mother was a perfectionist and would dot her i's and cross her t's multiple times before actually going forward with a task in front of her. Both sets of my grandparents were both married for more than that and shared the same oppositional pattern.

I always make the joke that two RB people in a relationship are like two sorority girls arguing over a guy. It's just a whole bunch of shouting and emotional tears, and nothing really gets solved. With two LB people, it's all about wolves battling it out to be the egotistical leader of the pack. Good luck trying to get someone to admit accountability in that pairing. It's the argument of seeing facts and then putting yourself in someone else's shoes. In order for a relationship to work, see it as a perpendicular line versus a parallel one. The intersection is important. One person's weaknesses in behavioral patterns complements the other's strengths. One person's thought process must be respected, and the other must feel internally valued in the relationship: logical versus emotional. The more you understand how your partner's wavelength frequency works, the more successful your relationship is. Try this methodology with anyone, and your arguments will become minimal and much easier to surpass. There must be a goal of balance. Two easygoing guys can't usually be together; one must plan to drive the ship somehow and the other to create a balance of spontaneity. Moreover, both individuals can't be workaholics because a lot of times, both gentlemen are so independently in their own world that no one makes the other accountable emotionally. We sometimes are not meant to date guys who are a lot like us.

I am all about embracing people as they are. It's so easy for us to make laundry lists. Most men that I interview only have a few nonnegotiables, despite age. The most popular are no smokers, men must be monogamous, no drugs at all, and sometimes someone who is completely out of the closet with no secret life. Well, working with a matchmaker, most of those things are already spoken for naturally.

I always have the younger "kids" who want me to match them with a Fabio Romeo too. Honestly, those guys are better dating on their own. I try to look at everyone like a person who will always have strengths and some weaknesses as an accompaniment. We now live in a culture where we meet someone and hope "they will change" or "get the hint eventually." I found myself being so guilty of having these secret expectations of someone and then being underwhelmed and frustrated. Maybe I should have just been honest, but then again, I also got the "Too soon to have this type of serious conversation" that would hinder my mouth from opening at all. There is some truth to this, to some extent. Trial and error are important here, just like a job, almost. Again, I hate to allude that a relationship is a job, but it kind of is on paper. You have expectations. You're required to communicate in a somewhat proficient, timely, and straightforward way. There is respect given to the other party and with some sort of follow-up. Hopefully, it's a job you look forward to coming to every day.

I look at differences in a relationship almost like a gauge. The "opposites attract" theory comes from differing interests more than anything else. However, if an introvert was a 1 and an extrovert was a 10, I probably would be reluctant to match a 1 or 2 with a 9 or 10. This preference is something I run into 40 to 50 percent of the time. A lot of men do not want to date within the same industry, even if there is a physical match. People are intrigued by differing lifestyles in a lot of ways. With someone saying "I want to date someone like me," they really mean things that are more surface rather than internal. Keep in mind a successful individual could be a proficient orator for a marketing firm or a guy who's a soft-spoken software developer. I have seen men that wish to meet men who would "ground them more," but this a mere difference between a 6 and a 4. In theory, the introvert would be consistently overwhelmed with a wider gap, and the latter would be bored or feeling tired that the progression of the entire relationship relies on his efforts solely. Think of it as a measurable sliding scale, which has only about a 3 or 4 in width. Sometimes peanut butter and chocolate are the best accompaniment to each other, but sometimes when the ratio is off, the satisfaction becomes a very heavy, uncomfortable indulgence.

In this light, I can take full responsibility on men I date being very intimidated by my lifestyle and line of work. I have had at least five men fall through the cracks in this theory of mine. These men are usually much more introverted than I, and we never wind up working out or meeting. They always make the same comment, that my life is so "illustrious" and "fabulous." My friends who tend to be more social than I, going to three to five events a week, probably view me as being slightly more introverted than them, and they even make the joke that I'll probably knit and drink tea before bed. Through humor, I can still not feel like it's overwhelming to me. It's important to find similar lifestyles in this since, after all, a lot of gay men tell me that they want a man who can mold well with his group of friends and hold his own in a crowd of strangers, if they are the more extroverted scale.

I also have noticed a lot of my past relationships have differing interests that definitely have caused a sense of intrigue. I love the fact that my partner can potentially have another interest that I might find weird or interesting. However, if this interest of his dominates his life, that is a huge issue. Think of it this way: if your partner lives, breaths, and eats rock 'n' roll—spending his week nights rehearsing with his band, going to loud concerts like AC/DC, loves kicking it with his crew—sorry, folks, this is something that probably won't change. He's going to want you to eventually like this because it's a huge part of him. If it isn't your cup of tea, then he'll have better luck finding his best match with the person who accidentally gives him a black eye in the mosh pit. You want the other person to enjoy what you feel defines you both on an internal and external scale. I especially see this with the yoga and vegan community, and devoutly religious individuals. Yes, most of these things being in the spiritual realm. You have to ask, is this something you see yourself molding into liking one day, or is it something that you would view as domineering at times? A lot of times, people view this as an extreme, and I hear this preference from time to time in initial interviews when asking what personality traits men don't want in ideal mates. It's almost like there was an overload of the circuit in the brain that causes something to feel overwhelming. In turn, men always want you to have a hobby of some kind, which shows that you can be independent and have a certain amount of social skills and positivity about life.

As of late, I have adopted this very East Coast style of communication, and I have been so surprised how many "Thank you for being honest" remarks I have gotten rather than "That's offensive." I wish we all could learn a thing or two about being direct rather than vague. Ambiguity yields confusion and then confusion can yield to something ominous in the dating realm. I've come a long way since my adolescent years, where a high school friend said I could be a bit of a pushover. I think in LA, the culture is quite the opposite. Meaning, we say we will do one thing and then disappear and mean the complete opposite based on our behavior. People like working with matchmakers mostly because no one can hide, and I take the bull by the horns for both parties. Everyone feels supervised, and there aren't second dates that are promised that actually mean the opposite. Our souls crave honesty, whether it's something we want to hear or not. We as humans are always searching for a way to become better in a general sense. Sometimes some can be a lot more sensitive than others, I understand, but this still doesn't negate the fact that we must hear what we don't want to hear to create synergy and growth in our lives. We start to become malleable in just about any situation in life that presents itself to us, whether it's predictable or completely unexpected. In this case, being more in the middle makes us more well-rounded and better daters. We become better daters, and better sleuths at deciphering wiring—which one needs to be cut and which one needs to be changed or even fixed.

Spiritually Awaken

One very rainy and wet Monday during the holidays, I was excited to connect with a dear friend in Georgia who was the wife of the youth pastor I grew up admiring throughout my adolescence. She had a seven-year-old, but was in her midforties. This was a blessing for her that was very unexpected. She had about two and a half more years before she would retire, having her fingers crossed, that her newly married daughter would provide her with grandchildren. As we caught up, I told her the excitement of sharing my book to the world, and she said something along the lines of "People are drawn to you because you are a man of God." She was rather excited with this news. I kindly smirked and told her that "I really try to do the right thing, and show kindness to everyone." She hasn't been the first person that has told me about the air I might emit. I have been told by men I have dated for years that I have good energy. I honestly view that as not just tooting my own horn, but as really acknowledging my strength as being a people person and having people feel like they can trust me right way.

I grew in quite the boxed religious area of the Bible belt. I felt church was just something I was supposed to do rather than something I wanted to do. During my childhood, what organized religion taught me was the ideal of being a good person, and that is simplicity and authenticity at its finest. Unfortunately, religion also played a huge part in closeting my sexuality, like many others. I remember having many conversations with God about why I liked boys, why I couldn't be like everyone else, why He made me this way. It was conversations like that that led to my depressive behavior and emotional imbalance. And imagine all this during puberty, when hormonal spurts make you feel suicidal. I remember telling my friends that "I shouldn't hate the sinner, but I should hate the sin." I honestly don't even know why I said that. It seemed more like a script than anything. This was what I was supposed to think rather than me actually making my own judgment call through an in-person connection. I hadn't really met any gay individuals, and the ones I had been exposed to were twirling batons in leopard-printed leotards on television, doing can-can kicks.

One of my very first dates as a gay man was with this preacher from about thirty miles from where I was living at that time. I found his story so fascinating, and it changed my outlook on religion forever. I met this guy at a local coffee shop after a long workday. He arrived nervous, like me, and we started chatting cordially. This man had everything on the outside: a fresh car he valeted on a sparsely populated weekday evening, a mansion with a staff (maybe this is me now exaggerating)—he had it all, it seemed on the surface. What everyone else didn't know I got to know first without being inundated with this picturesque fantasy. He was living a lie, and a really bold one at that.

He was a preacher of a very well-known church in his community. I imagine it was one of those megachurches. He did have a wife and kids, and if I remember correctly, his church was something that was generational, "in the family," as they say. He told me the story of how hard it was to balance his church life, his personal struggles, and his wife, who was terminally ill. He said he would stay by her side, every day, until she finally passed away. Deep stuff already.

He told me that he liked "fooling around" with men, but "that was it." This man was gay. Let's call a spade a spade. I was in the dead center of my identity configuration, and he acknowledged his, but in a very distant way. I actually remember feeling heartache for this man. How could he turn his back on everything for the selfish reason of him feeling like he didn't have to hide anymore? I almost remember crying for him. I was overwhelmed with his cemented boots he had to wear, which were polished so nice, but the weight of them was unbearable.

I first had my taste of religious experience years later after I moved to Los Angeles. I had never heard of this church before, but it was recommended by a roommate I had. I remember my first time was with a Bible in my hand and a tucked-in collared shirt, the ole Southern way I was conditioned to presenting. This church made me feel spiritually alive again. I was so drawn to the magnetic light it gave to my soul. Before I knew it, I was volunteering, got baptized again, and spent many years on staff. I even started tithing and lessened my work schedule to be more active in "my tribe" at that time.

One of my good friends I met through this church is truly a talented individual. She guides people to sharing their story through one-person shows. I remember one of the leaders asking her to remove herself from a leadership role because some of her subject matter was a little bit more liberal and unfiltered, mentioning LGBT subject matter. That was a little bit of the beginning of the end for me. I started noticing that people were just my friend when it was convenient for them. Deep-rooted friendships are what my soul thrives on. For me, everything seemed so surface. It was the "Let's hang out" thing, but I never heard from them again after numerous progressive attempts from my side. I couldn't count on these people if I was stuck on the side of the road with no one else to call. Heck, my paternal grandmother would always call her preacher when she was in peril. One time she called him because she literally got ran over by a car. Regardless, I started seeing a pattern; meaning, there was an expiration of this relationship some people were promising. I did not need them; they needed me. I didn't feel valued, and I didn't feel very much at home. I am a call-it-as-I-see-it type of person, and before long, I realized that I was just a marketing plan for them. They were using every intangible resource from me to benefit their mission. I remember sitting in the auditorium, taking notes, and I remember my frustration was creating a block for the permeation of the sermon. I was there just because it was "the right thing to do." I can do the right thing without the responsibility I gave them.

I remember struggling deeply toward the end of my initial descent in the way of gay men and women approaching me in the congregation who were new. I was the liaison and go-to person for how to get people connected within the community. What came to fruition was the ideal that this church thought that homosexuality "wasn't being one's optimal self." Although this church was progressive, they must be down with the gays. False. One of my friends mentioned to me that there was this probing personal interview about the next steps on becoming more of a visual representation of the church. I remember not being afraid to share who I was anymore. I refused to hide and remain in hindering silence. The church's stance came from the point of the congregation "walking together" with people who identified as a person in the LGBT community, which was a very surface smile-and-nod ideal rather than it being a belief that this person can be a Christian follower *and* be a LGBT person.

I remember writing my superiors a letter and telling them about my choice to remove myself because I didn't feel right about being there anymore. "I am lying to my fellow gay brothers and sisters" is something to the extent of what I remember mentioning. "I understand that you have to hold the traditional values of a church, but know that I have learned so much here and will continue to lead people to the light you showed me years ago." I remember having an intimate conversation with one of my superiors whom I had known for years. She mentioned to me about monogamy, told me about being the "optimal self" stance of the church, and also mentioned there was a "gay church down the road." I also got the inclination that she was trying to refer me to some professional in which one of her friends "was going through the same thing." Sometimes it's best to acknowledge someone in their passion, but sometimes you have to say good-bye, knowing that person is happy, but you disagree with that passion. I remember one leader rattling off a Bible verse and a couple others telling me they were proud of me, and we left it at that. No one contacted me after my proverbial exile. I guess I wasn't as important as they led me to believe. They preached community, but only from the surface. There was no tangible evidence to support that I was being treasured outside of those four walls.

I recall reading an article that said that these megachurches preach and create a "cool and comfortable" atmosphere with the preacher in skinny jeans, a fedora, and a V-neck. The higher-ups sometimes avoid the question of homosexuality in the church because it would cause people to feel like this proposed world of acceptance and creativity is a lie. Their safe utopia is now corrupt. Adam is sharing the poisoned apple to the exterior world. I can remember many members assuming that "Oh, I thought they—" The answer is no, and it isn't exactly a lukewarm standpoint.

A year or two passes, and my best girl friend is getting married. She was actually the first person to welcome me into this church community. She was also someone I came out to in the beginning and remains one of my best friends to this day. I am thankful that this entire experience led me to developing a strong friendship with her and many others. She felt the distance of her best girlfriends she became so close to in this church community when she started dating her now husband. This guy has no filter, and when people are taking advantage of him or her, he makes it very vocal. I guess people see him as very abrasive and obnoxious. It was disappointing to have these girls completely disown her after so many fond memories together. For them to show up at her wedding seemed like she had to force them to do so. I remember seeing her cry from the despair of being abandoned when this time should be so warm and exciting. They left her and never really came back. On her wedding day, one of the better pastors of this same church officiated their wedding. I had a brief chat with him before the ceremony, telling him why I had left the church and why I won't go back. He was struggling to be on my side of things, but it seemed he also had a couple of thick walls in front of him, distorting his honesty. Don't worry, you can't hide from me.

Another year additionally passes, and an unexpected kismet moment occurs on a flight home from JFK. Here was young man, a new dad, greeting me by my first name. He recognized me from this church. He shared his story to me, and he was in agreement with my assessment on his experience. This church was known to be a very creative space for a lot of artists to merge together. And the church would urge him to help and volunteer, but after a while, he was starting to feel used for his musical expertise. This happened again to my girlfriend's husband mentioned prior, in printing promotional materials for free. "For the good of the church" was no longer an equal mantra for both of them and myself.

I knew that this institution had certain rules and regulations to abide by. I understood, but with every decision comes certain consequences. Let's say they were in support of homosexuality. Then, every traditionally ubiquitous church would shun them, and people would stop attending. At least, this was the worst-case scenario that made the most sense to me. We live in such a progressive society in Los Angeles; I doubt that would ever happen. Come on, all these people are artists. They are no stranger to a gay person. Rules are rules, I guess. With their decision, though, there was the other side, where they would allow you to come, but would not support you. Going to soccer practice and not being coached or cheered didn't sit well with me and a lot of other people, I imagine.

I now attend a church every now and then that keeps me spiritually aware. This church was referred to me by the same individual that taught the one-person shows. This congregation comes from such an open place. One of their pastors was a partnered gay man with a newborn and another, and another being someone who is transgender. What was so inspiring was to see this individual's transition in front of his church congregation. He transformed vulnerability into inspirational confidence. I am in awe of the amount of love that is bursting from this man's heart, and it's infectious. I would much rather be with the non-mainstream kids than the cool kids at lunchtime. They always had better stories anyway and appreciate you for your heart and individualism.

When I am interviewing individuals to be matched, I notice that most gay men come from a lightly spiritual background in their current day-to-day, for the most part. It's the very New Age thing to do. I never worked for a company where spirituality was a requirement or even a quality people had requested for ideal mates. Keep in mind, I am not a spiritually driven niche service either. A lot of more spiritually aware men meditate or do yoga to find their balance. Heck, I run on the treadmill to find mine. Do whatcha gotta do. I also have had men tell me that their parents had exiled them based on their "choice" of a lifestyle and their conflicting religious viewpoints. Religion is a bit of a deep sour note for them, and I don't blame them at all. Just don't be one of those judgmental atheists, which never go well with a lot of people. Speaking of, I had this one client write me a verbose e-mail about how their date said ethereal terms like *heart* and *soul.* He told me this person was trying to oppress his fervent view-points. Whoa, buddy. Most people go the self-help route and go to certain authors that lead to that type of internal and external aware-ness. And then there are some who are die-hard Christians. It doesn't matter what you are; what matters is who you are. If you were to die tomorrow, what would your boss say about you? Your family? Your high school friends? The people you've only met maybe three times? Hopefully, there's an apparent correlation to all those relationships.

I sometimes think about what would be said at my funeral. I know it seems a little morbid, but it's more or less a measure of where I am at spiritually and how my heart is perceived by others. Most of my friends would agree that I was a good and supportive person, and that's good enough for me right now. This is a question I always ask when I interview people: "In five words, how would your friends describe you?" Maybe one day, I'll have a spiritual awakening, and maybe not. I was judged by my identity, and my optimal self is who I am now, a proud gay man who can maybe teach a thing or two to other gay men. When someone does you wrong, kill with kindness, and know that their actions speak for themselves and will get noticed sooner rather than later. Disagreements are about a learning curve. Sometimes people don't have the capacity to understand some deci-sions because they don't fully understand the situation. Whomever you believe, whomever you call your higher power, be able to share your authenticity with someone else, in the most endearing way. You won't regret it.

Dating Prejudice

In today's day and age, I find that people are starkly honest, sometimes abrasive in their ethnicity preferences in dating. One matchmaker noted that the type of racism is in our true core and that people genuinely believe their attractions are chemical. She argued that this preference isn't biological, that it's merely societal and institutional.

We all have our favorite cup of tea. I'll interview people who will promptly tell me "I am not racist" when I ask why they are only willing to meet Caucasian men. I'm in a subjective business that yields to bend a little. Mobile dating applications really create harsh stigmas against certain cultures. Our culture now is evolving into such a tiptoeing, sensitive one. People just need to calm down and not be so quick to point so many fingers and so quickly. Didn't your mother tell you pointing is a bad thing to do anyway?

Statistically, in my six years of matchmaking expertise so far, Asian and African American men rarely want to date each other but always want to date Caucasian men. This is something I hear quite a bit. However, Caucasian men list Asian and African American men as their least desired preference. So you can see that this prejudice is not only external but also very well internal. I'll have to admit, around sixty or seventy percent of the guys I remember interviewing to be matched with paying clients were white, white-mixed, or of Latino descent. I have nothing against Asian or African American men. It's almost about supply and demand, merely.

When I first brought up this topic, I had a young man respond with his personal testimony and truth in his journey of dating, and this abstained and obtained prejudices:

> "I'm black, newer to LA. I have dated exclusively within my race, but not entirely by choice.

I've been open to dating white dudes, which is different than hooking up, but I have found a few factors exist. Some of my black friends have said white guys in LA are, by and large, racist, while other black friends have dated white guys pretty much exclusively. It depends. I've found that the white guys I'm attracted to are boy-next-door [types] and don't tend to go for me or, at least, send the signals. That said, I've also been fetishized, only clearly wanted for sex, but yes, most of the time, I find myself overlooked by white dudes."

He added, "I love my [black] brothers! However, I have found, over time, a bit of cultural baggage, primarily as a result of factors many black men couldn't have controlled [like] upbringing. But I'm more than happy to date a black man who has his stuff together. I mainly wanted to date white guys because I haven't / wanted to try an alternate approach [or to] broaden my own horizons, not because I thought they were better. But as far as white guys, I am, for the most part, just as educated, traveled, culturally exposed, well employed, etc. [The] ignorance is as curious/painful as the blatant rejection. A guy on my kickball team last year, said, 'Wow, you're looking good! I never thought about going the chocolate route, but you're making me reconsider!' I'm sure it was meant as a compliment, but honestly, what am I supposed to do with that? [Being at] bars where you are one of very few people of color, if not the only one, you're so used to being alienated you sometimes forget it's happening as to preserve your own happiness or sanity. At the same time, I'll be honest. I do have some prejudices too. I won't say specifically, but there are ethnic groups I would be reluctant to consider, but mostly because of past experiences and cultural values I know to be true from exposure like approach to family, money, religion, etc. I've also found that 99 percent of the time, I'm just not physically attracted to some guys within some groups, and while that's not fixed and exclusionary of everyone in said group, it's my truth. I'm okay with that, and I don't think a preponderance to not see certain guys as physically attractive is in itself racist. Prejudices are different from racism. We all have them, and they can be changed."

I still am perplexed by our society, and we cannot even sometimes get past the name Muhammad, Salesh, or Tyrone. One of my coworkers disclosed to me, "I've had to change people's names or give them a nickname so that they don't get declined." As we grow as a society, we are becoming much more racially diverse, in genetic evolution and population growth. I wonder what would happen to most of everyone's preferences, let's say, in fifty years. Do you think they would evolve too? One of our other matchmakers at the office in response wrote, "We can say sometimes it's hard not to be influenced by what is culturally acceptable in Los Angeles. Despite diversity, people who are in the dating world are still looking for a commonality to fall back on, something familiar."

At the end of the day, it's all about how you present your preference. On a dating application, however, is that fair to judge anyone on these avenues? "No Blacks or Asians" seems a little abrupt, I agree. However, people use that for sexual and immediate physical chemistry, hence the get-to-the-point, succinct wording. That control group is not the one to draw conclusive evidence from. I personally have always had a preference of dating men who are or a combination of Caucasian, Middle Eastern, or Latino descent. I am in a big majority of men who prefer those similar to my age and build. I think it has to do with the fact that I grew up in a predominantly white neighborhood in my small town of Georgia. I simply didn't have exposure to seeking attraction anywhere else, because that was all I knew. It was engrained in me for years. I mean, I maybe knew three or four African American people growing up. Most of my friends where white or of Latino descent. I remember interviewing another young guy who said he spent a large amount of time in Japan and loved meeting Japanese men. A close friend who teaches my yoga classes told me she had mostly been attracted to white men. I asked her where she grew up, and it's somewhere in a predominantly white community in Minnesota. These instances support the theory and inclination of sociographic factors with ethnicity preference.

My theory is that physical, racial attraction and preference stems from how our brain deciphers facial symmetry based on how society has shaped us over time. I have come to find that a lot of left-brained men like sharper features because they favor symmetry and organization. This can allude to the belief that men currently dominant in their left lobe can be a bit pickier. Right-brained men are a little bit more of a mixed bag and can be a little less structured in their attraction patterns. Remember, things can change, though, when you are actually in a relationship. My theory stems from single people and which lobe is more active than the other from a long-term standpoint. Ask your friends who like the same guys as you and test my theory. I've tested it, and the data I have been receiving yields to a noticeable pattern. Sometimes physical stature too can correlate with ethnicities. Asian men can be more petite, while Hispanic, Middle Eastern, and African American men can be more stocky. These parts are anatomical, in some way, and this calculation is how our brain configures attraction in general. Yet the osmosis of society's impressions have wired us a certain way over time. African Americans have more prominent features, and the Asian race has more diminutive features. I have met a few Asian men I have found attractive, because their facial construction seem to favor my initial ethnicity preference. Our brains are all wired differently, but there are more similarities in them than differences in this topic. It is somewhat rare for me to interview someone who is open to all ethnicities. A lot of guys will also say, "I have never dated [that race] before and probably wouldn't start." However, I have met men who are very well attracted to personality traits, and that physical chemistry can develop over a period of time, regardless of racial preference. One of the guys I had interviewed said, "I know that I date a variety of men sometimes to try new things, and I generally end up going back to what stimulates me all around [as a whole] in the end. It's still good to try new things and see if those will spark a new interest in you." Don't judge a book by its cover, as I try to leave myself open to possibilities of flourishing chemistry. Sometimes I would engage in conversation with someone whom I was somewhat attracted to, but knew I would only be more attracted to them over time if they instigated more. I was more intrigued by how they conversed with me and was cognizant of their communication skills that might allow my attraction to grow over time. Most gay men are impatient and want instant gratification, though. I find this more in the millennial generation than any other generation.

Speaking from a long-term standpoint, I do feel a lot of men prefer to date from the same culture, as mentioned prior. I get that. Certain ethnicities prefer certain religious and family practices and bonds. Looks can be quite deceiving, though. Yes, I have tried dating all types of men, but I look at my myriad of experience, and most of it has favored the ethnicities listed prior. I'm sure you have similar stories to share. We are just creatures of habits, oy vey.

It would be wrong for me to not mention a generation gap prejudice here either. There's a lot of discrimination when it comes to age as well. I have gotten a huge brunt of it when I advertise speed dating events with a cutoff in age. At the end of the day, you're more likely to match with someone similar to your age. This will always increase in developing a strong bond. I do different age demographics from a supply-and-demand standpoint, as well as one to create realistic value. If I have an open speed dating event, the older demographic will usually choose to date youngins, and the younger guys will never choose them. It's a lose-lose situation here. I am not an ageist; I am a businessman who cares about the integrity of his events as much as he can facilitate. I cannot tell you how many men I have interviewed that told me their partner or all their friends just died around them during the AIDS crisis. Yes, the epidemic was devastatingly awful, and I don't want to downplay the sympathy in that struggle during that time. Yes, it was much harder to live openly from the lack of evolution in those previous years, but to allow this entitlement to supersede any areas of opportunity in your date practice can make you seem like you are above everyone. It can seem a bit unsolicited and cavalier. Not everyone was in the trenches at th forefront of that battle. Not all gay men were "out and about." I've met many gay men, including myself, who do not advertise their dating life out in the open. Yes, being a gay man is something that is a part of me, but it isn't the first thing I want you to notice. Sorry, and it's just none of your damn business who and what I do with my personal time. The "old geezers" and "trolls" who are groping the young men unsolicited at the club are the ones that give the others the bad reputation, just as much as the young gay with booty shorts, a man clutch, and a strip of fabric over his nipples do the same for the younger generation. Maybe those inappropriate people are just inappropriate *people*. The conversation should be about opportunity and conversation rather than a dismissal that strengthens a judgmental cliché. My mother always told her grade school students that "we don't hit, we hug." I hope and pray that future generations use more of their warm embrace with their heart rather than darting eyes from the standpoint of one's disparaging head.

I always like to say that if things don't work out in the dating realm, be the person that sets the bar for the other person. Too many times we can be a "what not to do" rather than a surprise of knowing there are still quality gay men out there in the world, despite things that appear trivial like race and age.

Gay Men and Their Archetypes

I am quite the perceptive individual. My perceptive memory will hopefully make me millions one day. I remember actively dating and starting to see correlations and patterns in certain types of individuals. I remember jokingly telling one of my friends, "We are not special." I didn't mean that as a detriment to being normal overall. Meaning, every gay man kind of falls into a certain category based on relationship history, generational influences, career profession, and overall personality diagnosis. I remember getting so frustrated when I was very actively dating in my youth. I remember I couldn't escape certain behaviors in men I thought I wanted. For instance, it was mandatory that a man had a stable career and was ambitious. He didn't have to make tons of money. With that, I noticed those types of men can be selfish, too busy, or too type A and never wanted to budge or compromise. Then, I turn the page and feel like I should date maybe similar to my age. I found that those men are flakey, not wanting to commit, or aren't as set in their career endeavors as much as I would have liked. Then, I would try and lower my physical standard just to have a nice guy and then come to find out that my physical bond wasn't strong enough to create longevity. It is about balance, and I am all about patiently waiting to find the right one for me.

Here's an analogy for you. This ain't my first time at the rodeo. I've been to too many, and as a spectator and aficionado of this sport, I've noticed that cowboys are similar in a lot of ways. Sometimes the beast he drives needs a little tuning. Maybe it's his form, or maybe the proverbial animal he is trying to tame is not the best fit. Sometimes we also have to take a gander into recognizing flukes as well as giving someone the benefit of the doubt. Let's explore the nature of each beast together.

All Talk, No Walk

I've met many of these in my experience. You know, the person that likes the idea of a relationship, but doesn't like to put forth the intended effort. That person who claims to have a go-with-the-flow attitude who also probably wrote "Seeing what's out there" in his dating profile. He's probably dating three other people besides you because he's taken light-years to reply about you asking how your day was going. Beware of someone who also says they "just want to have fun." Hey, I have no qualms about you being at that position in your life. I've been there, and many times. We're only human. However, come on, "fun" isn't staying up past midnight, drinking soda pop, and playing CandyLand. When I see that, sexual intimacy is usually involved. I wish these types of guys would balance getting to know other men equally and be respectful. However, most of these types of guys do not do that, so good luck trying to reel that fish in. I am all about dating multiple people if you are keeping things very light and casual, you know, a coffee date or happy hour here and there. By all means, you better be good at dating multiple men, but who has enough time for all that anyway in today's day and age? Since around the age of twenty-four or twenty-five, I will stand by the fact that every time I had felt deeper feelings developing with someone, I always was upfront with the other party. That's just fair and being a good person and holding yourself to the caliber of the minority.

I remember waking up at 4:48 a.m. one early morning after one of these guys ding-dong ditched me, if you know what I mean. I remember him telling me that he "really appreciated my honesty in my [online dating] profile." I also remember him telling me that he found me intimidating on our second date. At that moment, in those early hours, I felt alone and realized why his "great relationship" of four months didn't work out. He said he placed himself on a two-month dating hiatus, which turned into a four-or-five-month one. He also told me he didn't have too much relationship experience. When the person you love has held you, that changes your outlook and vocation forever on dating. My theory is that people who write "A person who won't waste my time" in dating profiles have dated a couple of these guys in his lifetime. He, simply, was victim to that person who liked to play the field. Let him play his sport, while I go to the concession stand and try to make conversation in line with someone who wants to listen.

My theory on these types of men is that they are like buoys: they are "open for anything" and are fine with floating around from ship to ship. Their aloof behavior can be frustrating, to say the least. Gosh, wouldn't you rather meet someone who's excited about creating a special bond right from the get-go? Why am I trying to convince someone that he should be ready to date for the long-term? Why the hell are you on a dating website? To me, it's almost like going to KFC and then the cashier being like, "Just kidding, we only have cheeseburgers." You should just know who you want if you are representing yourself truthfully, right? Maybe my idealism is a bit literal, but there is some sense to be made from my inclination. I am just not a gray-area person when it comes to something like this. There are too many subjective theories that come out of gray areas and usually cause more harm than good. I'm not sure how I would feel about a person being complacent, with a "whatever happens" scenario. I've interviewed many married couples before, and most of them say the same thing: "I knew he/she was the one. We just got each other. Respected each other from the beginning." They finally knew who they were, which opened up their passageways to allow them to feel unconditional love. And man, once you feel that, it's the most magical thing this world can offer a human being. They allowed themselves a sense of vulnerability, an option to fail, and if it did, it's all about going onward and upward.

I had another similar experience near Halloween one year. This guy had everything, the house in the Hollywood Hills, the physique. He was much older than I, and he lured me into his bedroom with such charm and rich conversation. I remember him with such a warm look on his face, saying, "You are going to stay here tonight." Shortly after some rather short conversation the days following, he told me "to allow things to happen naturally/organically" for us. I told him, he was going to never call me again because he wasn't putting forth any effort to get to know me. Um, he never did call me back. Duh, I ain't stupid. Ever since, that has been a trigger word for me. If I wanted something "organic," I would watch a pot of water come to a boil. Things take effort if you find them important. Drops mic. I've seen him recently, and he's plain gross, talking about how no one "wants a stinky kitty" on a popular dating application. Class act.

One of my first experiences dating an older man involved him treating me like his Ken doll. He never told me his age. I'll always remember his chic apartment, his Asian-inspired clothes divider, and his grand piano near his dining room. He didn't want me to touch him at all. He was perfectly fine finding his pleasure from being with me. Sure, cotton candy is awesome, but after the eighth serving, it can seem less appetizing and can make you a little ill. This man liked just the idea of being physical, I had come to find out, somewhat of a wolf in sheep's clothing. Man, was I fooled, thinking he wanted something further. He lured me right where he wanted me, until I snapped out of this daydream and realized reality and didn't bother tiptoeing around his proverbial tulips.

This archetype loves to date with the door ajar and half his boot already out the door. He says he's dating "smart," but intelligence and cowardice are two separate entities. He is also the person who will ghost you. You know, the person whom you've seen maybe once or twice, maybe seen each other naked, and literally he disappears. Cowardice is never an attractive quality, is it now? All the good daters would agree to give the benefit of the doubt. Maybe he broke his phone, maybe he's busy, maybe he was in a horrific car accident, or maybe he spontaneously combusted. We'll never know, will we? There is a difference, though, between experiencing a ghost and a relationship naturally fizzling out because "he's just not that into you." or vice versa. Ghosting is one of the most immature things you can do to someone, especially if you've been really invested for two weeks or more. Not many things make me start having vengeful heart palpitations, but this is one of them. I remember one guy disappearing completely after having a conversation with him about schedules. He was a spontaneous guy, and I am not. So we needed to come to a middle ground. He didn't want that, but instead of taking ownership of his own thoughts and concerns, he just didn't bother responding at all. As a busy working professional, via conversation with friends, I would assume if you want to date, then date with meaning and purpose. Have meaning behind what you say. "Keeping it casual" and "casual dating" have two separate meanings here. If you are actively looking on a dating website, then that means you want a relationship. If you like the idea of a relationship, then that's a different ball game. An idea and an actuality are completely different.

"I have been running errands all day," one guy had said to me in response to me saying, "Did you forget about me already?" I met him on a dating application, and it seemed we had such good, organic conversation. In the course of our three-day pause from the initial introduction, he changed his profile picture three or four times. Seems like he was just perusing, when his profile was quite appealing, saying things like "I'm a good guy looking for other good guys. Dates would be nice." I bet you an exuberant amount of money that his friends tell everyone that "I have this friend that is such a good guy, and he can't find anyone." Those gal pals should be looking at his conversations. If they saw what he was writing or not writing, they wouldn't be so quick to protect such an "eligible" friend. Excuse me while I find my pupils behind the base of my skull.

I had met this one guy near the holidays one year. I remember chatting with him on my way to the airport to LA from a popular online dating website. He was Latino in every way possible. I do not mean that racially, so calm down. He had close family ties, was an amazing cook, would stay up all night and drink expensive Mezcal from Mexico, and had a spicy attitude to boot. I remember us enjoying our time together. He would make fun of me and vice versa. His taste was definitely more refined than mine. I remember him looking at me as I ate my pizza like I was a savage. He was more of a fork and knife-er with a folded linen napkin, and I was the "Let me eat fried chicken with my hands like a starved redneck." I remember me being with him for a few months and realizing that our bond wasn't strong. Because we hadn't had the "Let's be exclusive" talk, I felt that I could still date around. It being early, I gave myself that pass. The thing though is that I crossed the threshold of being intimate with this man, and many times. I remember one night I got a little drunk after a friend's music event and went home with one of the backup dancers. That's a one-night stand for the books I wish to erase, but whatever. To be young and stupid again. Needless to say, it came out that I was also being intimate with someone else, and it also happened to be the same day he wanted me to meet his father, who was visiting. Um, can you say I should have shriveled and died right there? I was the biggest douche and asshole. The rose-colored glasses were forced on my face the best way possible, and lessons learned. You should learn from my mistake and have a little dignity, no matter what the paper definition may be. If you are cool with the guy you are talking to screwing other guys as you're trying to get to know him (mind you, after a month or two has passed), then please have a free-for-all. Most men with a kind soul will not go for this. Just use the "Do unto others" rule here. I now try to hold myself to a standard where I will always be intimate with one guy at a time, even though I might be passively dating others. There has to be a few dinner dates under our belt too before the envelope is all the way sealed. That intermittent period is fairly short for me, though, but as a majority, once that threshold is crossed in intimacy, all ties are cut with others. As I look at this experience, I was guilty of being this type of guy. I just didn't want to commit to him and wanted to play the field some more. Although, I think on paper, it must have seemed like I was dedicated to him. It wasn't fair to this guy that he saw something completely different. A year had passed, and I actually met with him to be matched with one of my clients at that time. It was weird, and we both voiced that; although, I can have a great game face. I had dinner with him a year later, after our last conversation, and he wanted to get back together. I think because I had grown so much as a man, my chemistry died. He'll make a great partner one day, it just won't be me.

I had met this one guy one summer on a popular dating application, and by far, he was the best match I had ever had on this platform. Ever. He was a young doctor who looked like a model and had one of the biggest hearts I had initially encountered. You would think I just struck some kind of jackpot. This is going to sound pessimistic, but I honestly asked him why he was talking to me. I felt he could do so much better. I felt he was a gazelle talking to a warthog. He said he found me handsome, and I guess that's all that matters. I just get very weary with men like that. There's always a reason why those guys are single. He lived a few hours away and apparently had dated someone in my same area, so I figured why not give it a shot since he was open to something not as convenient. He would check in on me from time to time and speak in what seemed to be Shakespearean sonnet-like visual metaphors about sunsets. I honestly felt he was from the movie *The Notebook*. He told me how he cried from his last relationship not working out because the distance was too overwhelming for the other guy, if I remember correctly. After six months of back and forth, my realism nerve struck fervently and asked if we were going to finally meet and that we should plan ahead. He agreed. Around that same time, he said he wanted to delete the app so he could have it "refreshed." Not even what seemed to be a few weeks later, he was visiting my area and didn't even bother to connect with me. Same thing happened two more times after that. Was I just used as a friendly face and engaging ear for what seemed to have been for months and months? Oh my gosh, I was the pen pal he never wanted to meet. Pfff.

In the end, these types of guys will sometimes say "There just aren't any good guys out there to date" with a smug grin and a nodding head. Believe me, there is some validity in this with some men. Sometimes online dating can be like finding gold rings in vats of sewage. And sometimes the first to complain is the first to blame. When people point fingers, there are four pointing back at you. These types of men can be lazy daters. "I like to hike, chill, not take life too seriously, and go on trips" would be under the 'Hobbies' section of their profiles. Whoa, you are so cool; I can't wait to grab a beer with you and talk more about your treacherous hiking adventurous while not taking it too seriously. Over time, in turn, they get in this perpetual cycle of dating many guys without making any progress, and they get frustrated. Then the self-proclamation light illuminates when they get screwed over, and they start looking for something more serious, with a new purpose and outlook.

Narcissist

The only word that comes to mind when working with these types of men is *egregious*. Nothing makes me hate my job more than working with these types of men. Some advocate that this type of person has a mental illness.

We've all dated one of these, I feel like. It's so funny; every single guy I had interviewed who'd fallen in love with one had the same "How did you know?" response when I guessed how they broke up. Let's mark that in the proven data pile. I had been in a relationship with a narcissist and came across an article about how they and an empathic person make a deadly combination. It really resonated with me how a narcissist could sometimes prey on someone who would always take accountability, because the narcissists would always claim to be a victim. I can see that correlation, and it's a scary exchange indeed. Every. Time.

I remember seeing a post about a date from a popular dating application gone wrong from one of my distant friends. This guy the entire time was trying to aggressively convert him to veganism. I myself have dated a person like this, and yes, I do eat a heavily influenced organic and healthier diet, but sometimes I just want a grilled cheese or a bite of chicken, and I don't want to feel like I just killed someone's domesticated friend or that I am poisoning my body. You do you, but don't blame me for not doing you. If your conquest is to change someone based on your standards and expectations, you are dating the wrong person, and this viewpoint is very tiring to hear.

I had a client that drove me absolutely bonkers. He was only in town like five to ten days out of the month. He was semifamous in his field and the biggest narcissist. Let me divulge for you. His "That would be great" mentality unnerved me to my boiling point. "That would be great [if you could call him and make him work around my schedule].” This client of mine also told me that he “loves to help and support his significant other in his career.” Okay, that's great on paper. What he meant by that was to make the decisions for them until the help was actually unsolicited. This client loved dating entrepreneurial men as well. The thing about those types of men is that they are very headstrong and independent and don't want or need help. Forcing that on an individual was not actually helping from a gratuitous standpoint but from a controlling one.

Sometimes you'll meet an inclusive narcissist. I remember hearing this type of narcissism distinctly on the radio as I was going into the office one day. This secret type includes you in the appraisal of a person's ego. Meaning, “Wow, I think we fashion-forward people should stick together. We need to go ahead of the line. Do they know who we are?” Basically, they are complimenting you as they are complimenting themselves. Sneaky, aren't they? Don't let that innocent charm fool you.

I presented a client of mine to this attractive young man once who was in a relationship when I last contacted him. Sometimes relationships can be a bit of a revolving door. We tango with someone for a moment, get out of the rotation, then get back into the section with someone again, and carry on. He responded to my e-mail to the extent of “I met the love of my life, and if that ever changes, you'll be the seventh person whom I will reach out to.” Um, best of luck to you.

Some medical professionals have viewed this as an apparent personality disorder. With this particular archetype, that person has to realize that they do not know it all somehow. They need to listen more and talk less. They should realize that they are not the only one in the driver's seat and that a relationship revolves around taking turns seamlessly. Hell might have to freeze for a millisecond for this miraculous event to occur. They must practice admitting they are wrong and know they don't have all the answers. They need to seek help. They need to be told to shut the eff up. They need to be presented facts and not feelings to belittle them to feel humility. They need to receive advice graciously instead of giving it all the time. Sometimes, narcissists have to learn things on their own when they feel that they have lost almost everything. Narcissists do not know they are narcissists. They obviously don't listen to other people, so don't bother telling them that they are an asshole, until they soften. They have to figure out that they are an asshole on their own sometimes. When narcissists realize they have no one who will rescue them, this usually can get them to get a grip on their life and decision-making. The thing about narcissists though is that they are great on paper, are amazing hard workers, and are passionate and charismatic about life. Don't let them fool you. Sometimes they are yet another wolf in sheep's clothing. They will suck your soul dry until you are left void of any deterrent conversation, and everyone will still view them as a "good person."

Finders

Sometimes men don't know what they want. If you know what you don't want in a relationship and want in a relationship, you've strode past this category. These types of men need get dirty, need to have their heart broken, and need to go through times that will shape them. Sometimes they have gone through those heavier times, and it's still lingering. They spend a lot of time figuring themselves out, and maybe the possibility of dating will get them to the mind-set of being solid instead of aloof. What doesn't kill you makes you stronger rings so true here, and that association allows keener perception. I see these men as walking through thick fog, not knowing who or what they might encounter. These men are almost *there* and are usually more genuine and kind than the other archetypes. You'll break up with them with a smile and a "I wish you the best" a lot of times. In general, sometimes these men can be a bit emotional and sensitive. Their life is in flux, so their internal stability can correlate as such. These types of men are the types to be erratic and explode into hidden expectations and wind up breaking up with you in a matter of a snap of a finger. Sometimes they cannot help the position they are in, and I've been here many times. I preach that similar life experience and pace have to come to an equilibrium to create a conglomerate effort for longevity.

I remember one instance with another guy where I felt like he was hiding something from me. So we had playful secret time, when I invited him over to cook him dinner. He was around forty and was just starting a nursing program. He had been a bartender for years, and I was like, he must be an actor, because that type of job for that long usually dictates freedom to do someone's true career concentration. I was correct, an actor—an actor in adult films. And by that,

I mean, like, a lot. Like think Tom Cruise of gay porn status. I was slightly shocked at first, but what our true demise was, was his emotional availability. He liked that I was communicative, attractive to him, but he didn't want to pull his weight. My theory was that he had to remove himself emotionally from true intimacy for so long that he lost his sense of true connection in regard to loving and creating that bond with someone. He needed to find himself before he found someone else.

I see a lot of men who are still not over their ex fall into this category quite easily. I am not one to judge. I will say it time and time again: you are not ready to date unless you feel like you feel you can be rejected, and maybe quite a few times. These types of men just don't know where they fit into a dynamic of a relationship. They are too malleable. Sometimes, they'll mold to exactly how their significant other wants them to be. I think Finders and Narcissists are a deadly combination for this reason. They are the more tumultuous relationships you love to gossip about behind closed doors.

I sit back and remember another amazing relationship, this one about seven to eight months in length. I am always a proponent of dating when you feel ready, when you feel like your feet are on solid ground. This man was a creative type and had such an amazing effervescence about him. I still miss him from time to time to this day. I had to think long and hard about why things didn't work out. He wanted to know every detail of my day and how it made me feel and almost like an emotional play-by-play of every moment in my day-to-day. This just felt unnatural to me, and he needed to date someone who was much more sensitive and in tune with that side of his personality. I don't think this is what really hit the nail on the head for me. This guy was in a crossroads of finding himself: one day he wanted to be in one career, then another, would get frustrated with his current situation, and then want to do something else, then go back again, and ask my advice, when I told him it hadn't changed. I wanted for him to be more stable and that instability wasn't something I was comfortable dating. I felt like my life was finally making strides to equilibrium, and his wasn't. I felt like I needed to balance him. This is in my personality, though. I sacrifice a lot of my energy for someone else, despite what it does to my mental balance. Maybe that was unsolicited of me. It felt right, though, to support him in any way I could, until it felt overwhelming. I think he needed to take a couple of years at his age, solidify something, and then open himself up to the possibility of something more substantial.

I also find that men in recovery fall under this category. I have dated all types of men in recovery from sex to alcoholism. These men have solid goals in their lives dictated by their healing process that must come first, before they think about dating fully in their own awareness. These men are too easy to change and need to have their feet on solid ground; otherwise, they might fall again, and sometimes their behavior can be just as wobbly as their day-to-day process can feel. I've heard the rule of thumb is for a person in recovery to not date for a year anyway. This a great rule. Dating is tough, so are you ready to feel the woes of it without impeding the flow of your goals that hold you responsible for yourself?

I have been here before, as I slowly raise my hand, as a fellow Finder. I find that these individuals sometimes have a hidden agenda. They can be fairly passive partners until they feel they are growing too fast too quickly, and then the pressure cooker builds too much and explodes. For people dating them, these breakups can be the worst at times: sudden, devastating, and frustrating, to say the least. Honestly, these men and women, aren't on your same level in regard to relationships, and that's okay. It isn't okay that they feel like they have been giving you mixed signals the entire time. It's almost like they give the external illusion of a positive trajectory, but their internal speaks much differently. Think of these men as interns trying to date an executive. Interns are learning, making mistakes, while executives know who they are and have gone throughout the experiences of life, which puts them in a different place of creating partnership.

I should coin the term "LA Slash." I find that most men who are in the mind-set of a serious relationship want to date someone with a definitive career path. I find that these men can be very outgoing and extroverted and can have overwhelming personalities. They also can veer into being labeled as "too in the scene." I feel straight men are a little more judgmental than gay ones, but I still have encountered this preference on both sides. The person I am referring to is a person who is great at everything. He's an actor, model, singer, dancer, stunt double, ventriloquist, professional mime, activist, server, chef…oh my gosh, I am tired. Think of Olympians. They have been training in their craft since they were five, and I think that makes them a valid expert at their craft. I think these types of men are still trying to find out what they are good at, which can be a big deal breaker for some. Hence, why a lot of times I don't interview anyone under twenty-eight. However, there are always exceptions to the rule.

I am not the type of person to become angry. My therapist has alluded to me that I should get an award for being the most composed person. One guy I had dated mentioned that he thought I was on suppressive medication when he first met me because I am that composed. There was one guy who made my blood boil, though. I remember writing him an e-mail one late night, awaiting his call for us to talk about things, and he, instead, got drunk and/or forgot. Needless to say, I am fairly good with words, and I called his continuous behavior "lackadaisical and unnerving." Whenever I would bring things up to challenge our relationship, he would reply that "he didn't understand," "needed time to process," or wouldn't even respond at all. He didn't understand why it was not the best idea for him to get drunk when my car's transmission completely bottomed out at the very start of one of my sold-out speed dating events. Wrong time, pal. Through us getting to know each other, I learned that he had been cheated on, and that probably severely frightened him. Enough to where he started on antiviral medication for HIV. I would introduce him to my friends, but he wouldn't bother to show me to his. I didn't want to seem pushy too, so I was trying my best to balance. This, of course, escalated to the point where I felt he didn't care about me or my feelings, because I really tried to make a conscious effort by trying to make his life easier: you know, clean his kitchen, take him out to dinner, etc. I remember telling him, "Maybe you need someone with less expectations, but I don't see anyone taking you serious if you don't have solidifying behaviors to cement the relationship, especially in the beginning." In my moments of heat, I thought he was just oblivious and tunnel-visioned. I felt he was in the process of balancing his personal fears and allowing himself to love again. I remember having a conversation with him later on when he was dating someone else, feeling that he had changed, and I felt really proud for him. Seems like he started finding his way, slowly but surely. I can say now that this fella is one of my closest friends, and I can't tell you how proud I am of him, on whatever journey life takes him.

I remember having an amazing first date with this one fella. Our second date was just as great too, which turned to us doing something PG-related after I had too many glasses of red wine. Our third date, however, took a big turn. I remember eating an omelet on a Sunday toward the end of the evening, and I remember thinking silently for a solid five minutes of how I wanted to phrase what I wanted to ask him, without me seeming "too much too soon." So I nonchalantly blurted, "What are you looking for in a boyfriend?" He paused for what was maybe five to ten seconds and said plainly, "I don't know." He continued after what seemed like several minutes, saying how he "just didn't know." *Oh, that's interesting,* I remember thinking. This man was in his late thirties. Um, you don't know what you are looking for, like, at all? I remember sweetly smiling and being cordial from his dialogue, but in my head, it was one of the brightest red flags I remember visualizing. It was like I was in high school again, and there was this intricate choreographed dance with a big marching band with every flag a shade of crimson flowing in the air. In addition, this guy was in a big crossroads in his career, but I was almost startled by how he didn't even know one thing, what he wanted. My theory is that he is one of those who hadn't really had any long-term relationships that gave him the things that he looked for in the long-term realm. He wasn't given the opportunity to create relationship responsibility: knowing what you can bring to the table and other things a partner can help you reach in potential through an amalgamate effort. Men who have that type of experience are very transparent in specific qualities they look for, especially in initial interviews when I am matching them.

In general, sometimes Finders are best matched with other Finders because they can get to a destination together and not even realize it. Sometimes this effort becomes cohesive and flourishes as a pleasant surprise.

Party-Hardy Uncommitables

This one is probably my favorite because a gay stereotype and its clichés exist in this category. I had a crush on this one guy from an event I was doing, and it's funny, I liked the idea of him, but in actuality, I knew it would never work. He was a mover and shaker. Every social media post was him with other hot dudes. One week he's in Seattle, the other San Fran, then Vegas, then Chicago, one weekend on a beautiful yacht, then he's at a heavily hashtagged red carpet event. Here's the thing, though, despite all his attractive physical and mental attributes, his life seemed way too overwhelming to me. I'm sure he is a responsible person and makes the time for guys he dates, but if I were someone first dating him, seeing him in different places with different muscular men, I don't know how I would feel about that initially. I'm fairly secure in myself, but that intimidation bug would start to bite, and those welts in my mind would fester. I mean, I would essentially be only seeing him, like, once a week.

This is a period in this gay man's life where he is exploring his sexuality for the first time and not willing to meet a version of Prince Charming. Men who are newly out of the closet or from a long-term relationship need to whore it up a little. A lot of these men really haven't gotten it out of their system quite yet and aren't able to date seriously. This is very relative to any age. In continuation, these types of men love dating in reverse, as I have alluded to in the past with a lot of clients. Hooking up and then realizing something with a little more emotional weight is there. Problem with that is, the build is initially gone, and then dating quick fix ADD can become a domino effect. It becomes more of a "thrill of the chase" thing rather than something with an apparent progression of relationship weight. They shouldn't commit, for the mistakes made in this latent period define boundaries, as well as characteristics in a person defines as attractive through communication. I've declined to work with some gay men for this very reason. They need to play the field before they even think about diving headfirst in the pack of wolves called gay dating. Hell, I've been in this limbo period more than once, and I am glad I was. I needed to get my mind and body back, and this process allowed me to get there without putting too much pressure on myself to be a certain way. I know I can be a great partner, if I am in that mind-set, but sometimes we need a dramatic pause to get back to the best version of yourself. Dating as a gay man can make you go from top of the world to bottom of the barrel real quick, and this is something you have to be aware of, that it doesn't necessarily give you the quick fix you desire.

I love a great happy hour, and talking with a Friday group at one of the most well-known gay bars in Los Angeles is definitely one of my favorite pastimes. One of my friends was talking about how his passive acquaintance who was dancing as a go-go was openly complaining about the quality of men via social media. This guy's problem was he wanted to be a heart when everyone looked at him as a spade. He was hot-bodied, had an accent, and danced for a living. Of course, gay men won't take him seriously, no matter if he had a degree from an Ivy League school and was the nicest guy on planet Earth. A spade is a spade, and that definition is how the gay society labels it, and sometimes that trivial label is like getting spaghetti sauce off a white shirt. It sometimes feels unavoidable and inevitable. There's always that certain residue no matter how many times you bleach it. This is not his fault, but he has to present himself in a way that doesn't stress the things that have given him that connotation of promiscuity and sex appeal.

I remember dating this one guy for some months. He was one of those guys making pop culture references and who would reference and quote nostalgic television characters on a daily basis, and still does to this day. I remember being attracted to his fun and vibrant personality. I liked that he was really social too. I remember me moving my schedule around to meet him after an event I was doing one evening days in advance. For those of you who don't know, parking can be an issue for a lot of areas in LA, but among the worst are anywhere near Hollywood Boulevard or Koreatown. He lived near one of those hellholes. I remember us having an argument over what was labeled as "tentative" plans. We agreed on this time, this isn't tentative, but nice try. I was like, didn't we plan this date? Couldn't you have let me know hours earlier? He didn't take ownership of his actions, and that's when I knew I was dealing with a little boy and not a man. Some people might refer to this type of guy as having some symptoms of the Peter Pan syndrome.

I also remember hooking up with him maybe a year later. Oops. Dumb mistake. We met again years later, and we realized that we are just different people now. I love seeing how compatibility can evolve, so the premise of "Timing is everything" rang so true to me.

I hear my thirty-five-plus clients always talking about how they always run into trouble with boys—yes, boys—under the age of twenty-five. It's perpetual, and I always say, "You know better." I find these types of guys do a lot of convincing rather than showing an actuality of that infamous and proclaimed old-soul ideal they claim to be dating. These youngsters are almost like ticking time bombs and can be erratic and unstable. They are texting you like there's no tomorrow, are emotionally needy, and want you to take care of them although they sometimes proclaim independence. Sounds like such great fun in the sun, yes? These men are Adonis sirens who want you to drink their sweet nectar and for you to hear their alluring song because you are so enamored by their youth, vibrance, and external glow. They are a fusion of this archetype and are "All Talk No Walk" masters in disguise with dirty, dirty thighs. This is a mere fairy tale, and apologies in advance, it usually never has its happy ending.

I have met a lot of gay men, and for every ten guys I meet, probably 9.5 of them mention not being "in the scene" and wanted that in a partner. On average, guys looking to settle down might go out once or twice a month to their local gayborhood. Think of your social media posting as a catalogue of the representation of who you are. Your consistent #SundayFundays of you drinking in a T-shirt that looks glued to you, all your shameless shirtless selfie postings about the progression of your new workout routine, and your consistent referral to yourself as a *she* or *her* tells an important story that is very unforgiving.

These men are also heavily addicted to the succubus of mobile dating applications. Someone once told me that "[Dating] apps are like window shopping. Just because something looks nice on display, don't mean it will look good or it will be worth the purchase. Chances are it won't last long due to wear and tear." Someone replied saying that "it's like fast fashion. Who needs to commit to investing in quality when you can throw it away and get a new one?" Yes, you heard me; a succubus is something that basically sucks the soul and life out of you. They are also the first to complain about being screwed over, almost like an eye-rolling broken record. I always preach that you use these applications how you want to use them, but these men aren't using them to date. If they do, they are lying to themselves and you. Listen, no one deserves half the awful casual encounters on those avenues, but in my experience, those things are extremely addicting and, to me, cause one to remove himself from feeling true intimacy. You are dealing with true human emotions here: it's a different mentality once you cross your own proposed boundaries.

I remember my first circuit party in San Francisco for Gay Pride one year. This would be my first and last experience. I can see how this scene can be addicting, almost like a drug. It's totally a "sex, drugs, and rock and roll" feeling. Um, you are not missing much. I still remember the putrid smell of molly (I've never even seen it in my life), sweat, and mistakes. To me, it seems more numbing than exciting. Take a big dose of reality and maturity. You just can't be over forty-five and partying until dawn anymore *like this*, operative words. How would your peers see you if you were in the dead center of a business meeting? You are not as young and hip anymore like you were ten, twenty, or even thirty years ago, and that's okay. There's a way to have fun in a more controlled environment. Then again, some people would argue that I need to live a little.

Don't be a cheater. Think of it as a felony to your love life and an uncommitted label you may never be able to remove, or be prepared to explain yourself in a very honest, accountable, direct way. Think of it as that tattoo you wish you avoided on Spring Break of yesteryear. Sure it happens to people, but sometimes that decision will come back to haunt you when you apply for new prospects. It's not worth drinking and driving just as much as it is for the act of infidelity. The consequences from both those actions can sometimes be irreversible. For the other party, it's the issue if they would ever be able to have the opportunity to build a strong foundation of trust with you. On an aside, some traditionally minded men might label you as uncommitted if you are in an open relationship too. Not my judgment call, just speaking from experience here.

Busy Body

Bottom line, if you have to try and convince me you have time for a relationship, you are lying to me and yourself. Get a grip on reality. Actions speak louder than words. You ain't fooling no one. Stop this deep conversing via text because you don't have time to meet in person. Gosh, am I guilty of this. Sometimes, after a call hasn't been returned more than once, and texting is the only thing that works, that is usually a telltale sign. You need to talk to your significant other every day. Having someone casually text you in the morning, during the afternoon, and at night is normal. The middle can be dropped when there has been a strong foundation established. This isn't needy or labeled as "codependent on your phone," this is just how a budding relationship grows into something with more weight. This is about creating the best first impression possible. This is a fair expectation, and usually when a bare expectation is not being met, the relationship fades to black. You should care about his day, and he should care about yours even if it's monotonous and boring. This is dating maturely. Do you sense a sour note in this one? If you are not able to do this, just don't date, and that's okay.

On the other end, being a Busy Body might not be a bad thing. I get it, sometimes you have to ignore things to make things happen for you and your career, but there is a sacrifice involved. One thing for another. The thing that irks me is people presenting themselves as available to date but actually don't have the time. You shouldn't be dating anyone if you feel like you don't have time to text someone two or three times a day. I cannot tell you how many people who have tried to work with me have said that they need six months to be in a proper dating space. There are no qualms or bad intent here, just don't complain about being single, buddy.

I remember at one point having to reschedule for a date a couple of times with this one individual I was interested in meeting as a date. After saying he would get back to me multiple times on these tentative plans of his, after feeling like he had flaked on me yet again, I told him exactly what I did to make myself available. "So I made arrangements both yesterday and tonight to make myself available for us to meet. I rescheduled a conference call, cut time short with a friend who is ill, and rescheduled my friend to meet me later for my party this evening. I think I am getting the wrong impression of you. Let's regroup in the new year if the stars align for us to meet again." He replied, "I appreciate your thoughtful answer, and I'm sorry. You're right. I am not a flake, but I've been a bit overworked and very scattered this last week. We can regroup again in the new year. I'm sorry about your friend, and I hope he/she feels better." Then there was a beat. "God, I'm the guy I complain about." My response, rather terse wrote, "No worries, happy holidays." At this point, I threw him a bone but also stood up for myself. If he wants to take me out, he could come to my area, and do it on his dime. I felt I had already done too much to a complete stranger and was genuine and kind. I did my part; he didn't do his. Fast-forward a month later, and we did finally meet. We had a great brunch date, and he was very intrigued by how intelligent I was. I don't think I was his "normal." I had went on a hike that day and afterward met up again with my friends, and then we joined him. All of his friends were at least ten years younger. There is nothing wrong with that, but case in point, these types of friends wouldn't be telling him to go for it and hold him accountable to his own dating trials and tribulations. Maybe it's a *you* problem rather than an everyone else. Crickets from him after I had checked on him the next two days. I felt there was nothing I did wrong. Seems like this was also an "All Talk No Walk" kinda guy. He is responsible for his own dating woes, even though he did think I was "intense" but said "Good for you" for standing up for myself during our first interaction. People like him are frustrating to see because I once again see a potential, but not an actuality, which is important.

I recall one of the very first guys in our database would tell me how he was ready to date again after a short three-month relationship. I remember trying to set him up before that relationship and remember how much he sabotaged his dating life by never responding to my e-mails and texts about him following through with dates and how it sometimes seemed like years to get him to confirm his availability, etc. If I was pained by this, I know a person he would be trying to date wouldn't give him half the amount of time and patience I did. His feedback from the last guy I tried to set him up with was "Our texts really didn't go anywhere. [We] didn't really hit it off." I am done setting this guy up. He just wasted my time and the other's time. I'll put him in the Busy Body category and wait until he can make the time to make himself available to date. He was an LA Slash as well. Go figure.

This might be very nitpicky of me, but this needs to be mentioned. I am finding more gay men are addicted to their animals than most people. I get it; you are single and want companionship. You have an animal to make you or allow you to become more aware and responsible. Maybe you always need the out when you are feeling it's past your bedtime at a social gathering. Having a friendly face greet you after a good or bad day is a rewarding feeling. However, I don't care to see your dog eating, sleeping, playing, making a cute face on your couch pillow, all in the same day via social media. One of my coworkers at one point said that to make yourself more eligible, you should get rid of your cat. Yes, a lot of people are allergic, but with that aside, balance is key. The one thing for me personally is never feeling like my significant other could spend the night at my place, because he felt he needed "to be home" or "to feed his dog" or "take him/her out." Listen, I am a huge advocate of your furry friends. I am that person on social media who posts videos of baby hippos and sloths. Anyway, I will say, at times, I was overwhelmed because I thought this person was way too busy with his job, social life, and his pet and me respectively. Don't be offended if the guy you really like has a problem with that time differentiation over a long span of time. He just wants to be a priority too. Find a good dog sitter, and make your date think you have purposely made time for him. After dating three men in a row devoted to their pets, I placed a note in my personal dating profile passively requesting no pets in men I wish to date. I had a guy message me a bit perplexed, but after mentioning what was written prior: "No, totally does [make sense]. I can understand that. I think for a good while I was very hesitant and reluctant to leave my doggies alone, and I can definitely admit that I had the same tendency to want to do things close-by or at my place. I asked because at some point, I do think it became a problem, but it was not pointed out to me. I've definitely changed my habits since and realized I need to make an equal effort to make things work. Thanks for that insight, good to know that the littlest things do make a difference. Also, just so you know, someone willing to make that extra effort for someone's pets, to me at least, is awesome. I know it's not always fair, but a mutual in between is great! Good chatting! Have a great day."

Also, I've met men who have this travel bug, and man, that critter took a huge bite and hasn't let go. I've understood these men having that adventurous, traveling-gypsy spirit, but a lot of men looking from the outside view you as not having any weight and being way too busy. I remember passively talking to this one guy for months who was taking at least three trips, it seemed, in one month. "Travel is a huge part of my life now," he said to some extent. He even invited me to experience New Year's with him in New Orleans. I told him with innocent sarcasm, "When you can make time for a regular date, I'll consider it." He wrote, "Fine. You win." Never heard from him again. Men who are seeking longevity want to meet other men with a little bit more of an established weight from the get-go. Instead of a tree, you'll seem like a leaf to most people. That is neither good nor bad; it just depends on what the guy your dating thinks of it. To me, travel to your heart's content, but when you are ready to date, slow down. Your bucket list will always be there and so will the places you want to visit. Plus, isn't it better to experience those things with a companion?

I've met men in their later years that have told me that they dated mostly in their twenties and started focusing on their career throughout their thirties and into their forties. I preach about divorcing your job all the time. Why would I want to apply for a law firm if I have no schooling or law experience? Same thing with dating with no résumé, you are a red flag to a lot of people. It's almost like never being married by forty as a woman in the straight world. I get it; we gay men can sometimes have this perpetual nature to be successful and to be validated internally or externally. What the feeling of true love does is it validates us metaphysically, something that stays with us for forever. Success can come and go, making it less solid and more unpredictable.

Busy Bodies can also use mobile dating applications heavily over the long-term. If I look at all the men over their late thirties I had dated in the past, I would say 90 percent of them I met via one of those avenues. Most of them being busy all the time and suffered from having no time to commit to someone in the long-term realm. It seemed like something else on their list. Finders normally find their way, and Uncomittables have few standards and sometimes will go out with anything with a penis. This is mere sarcasm, of course. The much busier fellas are looking because they are lonely and because those avenues offer 24-7, 365 style service. They basically use them when they have those few free hours, which is normally on late nights or while traveling. When I was actively looking on those types of things, I noticed these types of men can only afford the time to do something very NSA rather than something that will last a little longer.

I find that they offer roadblocks continuously in the laws of connection, especially on the first meeting. Busy Bodies need structure and need someone to reel them in; otherwise, the other guy will never feel like a priority and peace out without giving you a chance.

"Hey, are you free Friday for a drink?"

A Busy Body would dismiss this and say, "Sorry, I already have plans."

"What about this weekend?"

"Unfortunately, I am very busy this weekend."

"No worries. Let me know of some time the following week that will work, and we can plan in advance."

"Let's reconnect on Monday and decide. I am unsure of my schedule."

This typically is followed by a "Work got busy, and let's reschedule." Geez, the guy on the other end, I hope he is patient and forgiving. Instead, why doesn't the guy just offer a solution of some kind? I find aloof behavior very annoying. "Thanks for the message. I'm busy this weekend, but what about Tuesday after work? Seven p.m.? There's a great spot near the Starbucks that has a good wine selection." Boom. You just made the sweetest lemonade the other fella can drink. Be proactive and less inactive to create less of this label.

Eager Ernest

There's nothing more entertaining to me than a man who is single one week and then swooning about the "love of his life" a week later. It's almost like Cupid's arrows have run out because of the trajectory those arrows, hitting one spot, and repeatedly at that. He is the guy where you would always tell him, "Wow, that was quick." He is the oversharer and the person that falls in love with anything that breaths the slightest chivalrous effort. I find that these types of men are usually younger or are those "forty-five going on twenty-five" types. On the other hand, I've found that some men have that instant connection and have really successful relationships. However, that is in a slim minority.

I am one of those types that always fly under the radar, but I usually am very proficient at putting pieces of a puzzle together. One of my favorite stories about this type of person involved a younger man dating someone probably fifteen years older than he. I received an adorable e-mail one day, updating and thanking me that this younger gentlemen had met another guy in our database, on his own, and that he was really happy and excited. A couple of days passed, and his Romeo he was referring to sent me an e-mail telling me that he was still actively dating and would love to be considered for our paying clients. Just a day or two later, I received this e-mail, "Unfortunately, I broke up with my partner recently after months of fights, being the only committed person and being selfless." That next Monday, I got another e-mail from the same guy, "We got back together on Saturday. No more breakups. Sorry for the back and forth." An additional two months passed, and this same younger gentlemen sent me an e-mail entitled "New Chapter."

"I broke out of a toxic relationship, thank God. A lot had been learned and many new experiences [I went through]."

I don't want you to confuse eager with desperate. The problem from working from the outside to in is that you never really get to know the internal construction of a person, just the physical. It's merely the nostalgic effort of dating that is so infectious. Trust me, the physical can only get you so far. As you can see, sometimes these men will ping-pong around and be their own enemy and the main cause of their frustrations. These men can easily go into a dark, viscous cloud of dating and sometimes only find physical love. They usually come out not as jaded as when they entered that time of their life, initially, as time progresses. They learn a little from their behavioral mistakes, fingers crossed.

These types of men haven't really found their relationship independence and how that equation can give them the best result. I always like to say that you are two independent entities working dependently together. You have to be your own person, but you also need somebody to steer the ship every now and then.

Have you ever encountered one of those gay dudes who incessantly tells you they "have no trouble meeting people," in the most pompous way possible? Can this person also be narcissist? They're so eager to puff their chest in their Casanova clout. All the better daters don't even say how many people they have dated successfully. The problem with collecting so much fool's gold is it makes you a fool. It's the ones that date knowing where the specks of gold are and how to recognize them versus the impostors. It's about quality versus quantity—always.

The Delusionals

I love when I get a forty-year-old client who says, "I don't have much relationship history." They are either a Busy Body, a Delusional, or worse, both.

Delusionals are those people who feel like "they deserve" the perfect person, and a lot of times, it can be so out of their own ball park. They would rather be single forever than to settle. Let's face it, I am attracted to athletic guys. Some days you can see my abs, with a good social media filter, and then I think I am Mr. Olympia, and I can get anyone I want. False. I veer sometimes on gay skinny fat, and I am fine with that.

One of my fairly handsome clients was very guilty of this and drove himself into a depressed oblivion. I have worked with match-makers before that love to use the 1-to-10 scale, which I hate because it's absolutely very surface. He told one of the matchmakers at our office that he didn't care "if they collected trash" for a living, as long as the other guy was attractive. He told us how he wished he could change, but it wouldn't "be happening anytime soon." This man was also newly gay, so pretty, shiny things, of course, appealed to him in the immediate sense. In this case, he was a solid 8 looking for an 11. Sorry, pal. People want to date people like themselves. And people who are ready to date have done their homework past the surface, and a lot of the time, looks aren't as important as a guy who can hold an intelligent conversation and just show up to the date altogether.

This particular archetype is so prevalent in speed dating. I have moderated several of those events in my day. I found that the more unattractive guys would have the worst results by picking the hottest guys that pick the least amount of people. They would then e-mail me, declaring how depressed they were that they "didn't get chosen," like they were the last person to get picked on the kickball team.

Sounds like these men had expectations that caused them their own dating demise.

"I know what I want. I am a very visual person. Looks matter to me." You aren't all that and a bag of chips. And my new favorite, "I want to meet someone who takes charge. Like really take charge, aggressive." Calm down, honey, your sexual domination innuendo is unnerving to me, considering what you seem to bring to the table. I won't even go into this story because I am afraid he'll sue me. He was cray cray. Both barely had any type of notable relationship experience. MmkayBye.

I'll always remember a client I had for a bit that was almost impossible to match. He only wanted to date white men. Okay, there went over 50 percent of our database. Second on his priority list was absolutely no pets. Apparently, he had some anxiety from them, and sometimes I would have to ask members of our database the size, weight, and breed of their furry four-legged friend before any type of consideration was made. I always try to be very understanding of preferences some men have, no matter how obscene they might appear to normal people. The thing about LA gay men above the age range he requested was if they were single for a while, had a stable career, they would have a pet of some kind. It's almost like a given, simple clockwork. LA men and their pets are no joke. He also wanted Jewish. The thing about LA is that we are not the religious breed. I am from the Bible belt, so I get those types of people right away. Of course, pockets exist everywhere, but my theory is that because LA is such a melting pot, people kind of accumulate their own spirituality as they go along. Most people are spiritual, but I wouldn't say as a whole we are devout one way or the other. He also wanted them to be educated, him having went to a very prestigious school. Just to throw things in there, he preferred men with no facial hair. So as you can see, his search was challenging, and if anything, him working with a matchmaker made him realize that. Thank goodness he had a team of matchmakers to try and do the sleuthing beforehand. I felt he wasn't meant to be in Los Angeles to be successful. He moved somewhere else for a job opportunity and probably has had much better luck through a personal search in his new territory.

I remember getting an e-mail from a gentlemen in the Midwest about his preference for young men. But like young, young, barely legal young. I mean, there's no way I could help him, but I was very intrigued by his thought process. He was trying to convince me that he wasn't a pervert in any way, but he just wasn't attracted to anyone else. I defined his infatuation as him wanting to protect and "teach" these boys about intimacy and life in general. But yes, he would need to go to a medical professional to explore that further. Here's the thing about having a huge gap in age: younger men can see you as a having a father complex. They like being taken care of, whether they are blatant or not, and you feed that unspoken desire. I was guilty of this when I was young and stupid. It would be interesting to study both ends on how sociographic factors and the ideal of a family unit and how it was defined with them throughout childhood. Most people would see this as something humorous, i.e., "Yeah, right, that'll last. Is he at least having fun?" I try to stick to that rule both personally and professionally. His delusion was the fact that reality was exactly what it was, and there was nothing he could do about it. He couldn't change societal norms and laws of mutual attraction for the purpose of longevity.

Delusionals need to realize that their problem is a "me" issue rather than an external one, as this again being a great prescription to get through other archetypical periods. Delusionals can also show narcissistic behaviors too. Maybe they should drop their expectations to actually get notable dating experience. If they find that type of "perfect man," anyway, how are they going to be able to effectively court him?

Negative Nancy

Someone once told me that in dating, "it's your job to look for something cool in everyone you meet; it's not their job to show you." When people sit across my desk, telling me that they deserve this person, that can either be an sweet route or the road a person takes that can set themselves up for failure.

I hate to say it, but I suffered with this one for a while. Gosh, I was so fed up with dating and was so quick to judge. I have softened quite a bit now. I felt like I was a very mature young man, living in a world with the expectation that I must be like "other guys." This made me frustrated.

Another one of my first official dates was a guy looking me dead in the eye and telling me I was going to cheat on him on our second date. Um, ouch. This guy is still very single and publicly adamant about his hookup "dating app" trials and tribulations via social media. I've also met many men that are either overly sensitive or were tired of meeting men who were negative all the time. Seriously, the guy that has a comment about everything. Can we at least try to be congenial for a second? If this human is mean to the waiter, doesn't tip the valet, or the conversation seems a bit pessimistically heavy, chances are the furrow of his brow needs to relax, and not on your time. In that, there is more of a deep-rooted issue that a matchmaker cannot diagnose.

These types of men, I have noticed, can be hyper left-lobed in their brain. So much so that they can seem almost cold. I started chatting with this guy for a few weeks. When we were planning our first meeting, he asked me how I would like to proceed. Was I being casually reprimanded in a business setting? Okay, no worries, I could smiley face my way out of this weird feeling. I had gotten to know this other guy before him, and I felt things were getting a bit more serious, so I cut off ties with him. I told him I just wanted to be honest and didn't feel right dating two guys as I felt one was leading into a more romantic direction. Things didn't work out, and I reached out to this same individual a week later. He did not like that. He called me "flippant," said I "treated him like a yo-yo." Geez, I asked him, should I have kept my mouth shut and just went on a date with him? I get it; the timeline was a bit nominal. Through more on-the-brink-of-condescending conversation, he informed me that he "tries to not invest too much into someone [before they meet]. It's too hard and tiring to then be disappointed for whatever reason." All right, sounds fairly logical. In the course of a few weeks, I initiated 90 percent of all the conversation with him. He waited, which seemed like years, to respond. He told me that I "seemed" cute and did a "lol" once. He never showed any common interest in how my day was going. He also told me that the qualities I was attached to were buzzwords like *integrity* and *balance*. Those are pretty straightforward, pal, living in a land of flakes, fakes, and workaholics. What I should have done was calculate all my response times versus his and my amount of words versus his and gave him his own dose of his robotic medicine. I told him there was a difference between getting to know someone via text, which I am against, versus putting your best foot forward and reciprocating. In the sea of judgmental LA gays, it's a must.

I met this one guy at a local bar off NW Twenty-Third in Portland one time and enjoyed getting to know him. I could tell right from the first moments of meeting him that he had quite the chip on his shoulder from his personal dating experience. And after telling me that his date he just went on was on his phone the entire time, checking his phone for other dates, and also telling me that personal hygiene is an issue with Portland men, I kind of don't blame him for his viewpoint. He also mentioned how he showed up on this one date a week ago where the other guy said he was parking, and he never showed up. Wow, no wonder the idea of dating probably seemed less than enjoyable to him. My first impression was that he wanted a hug rather than get to know me.

One of my older clients needed to get the award for the Most Negative Nancy. He felt he was better than everyone we were sending him, and it almost felt like "he was doing us a favor." The dates we would send him on would sometimes rave about having fun with him, and some would say he was a "bit too conservative." I felt that was someone saying they felt judged. He would be very short and say he had nothing in common after most of his dates or something like "Funny, no romantic connection, let's move forward." He was not warm to us once although we had given him around nine dates in the six months we worked together. I think if you have an open energy and heart, you can find something in common with just about anyone. His haughty attitude made me cringe, and I am one to appreciate a to-the-point response. I felt people also picked up on that energy, which stood in the way of his true happiness. I should mention that he had also been single for over fifteen years. He would call us at work just to complain, like for a half hour. He would get his panties in a wad from a date being rescheduled. He would get mad at me for not knowing every detail of his date's life, and it's my fault I didn't "warn" him. He felt that he was thirty years old, even with him standing in front of me in front of my desk, and saying, "Look at this, I take care of myself," with an up and down hand motion, pointing to himself. He would constantly remind me how he was in good shape and had been for thirty years. De-lus-sion-al too, aren't you? Couldn't we just ride the wave naturally to the shore for a date rather than going down ravenous rapids? I tried to give him a life vest, but it seemed like even the brand of life vest wasn't going to be good enough for him. Killing him with kindness was actually killing me when I had a cringing smile that would make my molars crack. He needed not only a piece but an entire realism pie. He was his own worst enemy. He was so negative because his expectations were unrealistic. He was judging things too quickly and would rattle off his online dating profile disappointments at the drop of a hat. I'm done. At the end of the day, you are your age, a number, and that matters on both ends, in a way.

I was trying to get some last-minute attendees to a speed dating event I was running and got this reply: "I give up on dating after trying everything for three years. Not like it was in my day—sixty-one years old isn't working in LA and online." So, um, wouldn't you *do a* speed dating event then? He made Eeyore look like he was high on Helium and doing cartwheels with a Ribbon Dancer down Sunset Boulevard. Listen, I get it, we've all been there and been so jaded. We have been failed so many times. However, when we date these types of people, they are placing too much expectations on someone, and then once a person doesn't meet them right away on their time, they get upset. I could say this exchange can happen in other archetypes. For me, to fix this, I had to lower my expectations of others. I didn't lower the expectations of myself though. Practicality goes a long way. If I felt like you had some reasonable red flags, I wouldn't string you along. I'd let you go sooner rather than later. I knew I was a good dater for the most part, but I was confident to say that a lot of men do not date like I do. That alleviated some pressure in my proverbial expectation pressure cooker. I went from a Negative Nancy to a Pragmatic Paul.

The Keepers

Although a lot of the archetypes have a negative connotation to them, this one does not. My theory is that Finders become Keepers, once their way has been found and their character has been solidified by relationship experience. This person has done their homework. This person has dated a lot and picked the good pieces of their dating puzzle as they went along and has started to create a beautiful mosaic of opportunity to connect with someone wholeheartedly. This person knows who he is, almost on a metaphysical scale. These people are generally more open and, I find, make the best strides to a happy, loving relationship. These people are ready to be swept off their feet. These men are okay to fall or trip along the way with a smile.

When working with these men, I find that if I can't introduce you to the love of your life, I can help you get there based on the human experience of interaction. I root for these men, and I graciously hope that they meet someone worth their time because they are at that place in their life where that is all they need to feel complete. Sometimes Keepers can become quite jaded because they've done their work, and they feel others are not on the same level. Sometimes Keepers try too hard and get defeated, but remember, patience is a defined virtue in life, and sometimes not having as many expectations can give you a sense of surprise and elation once you encounter the one. The universe, or whatever you call your higher power, will give your due diligence if you wait.

One of my favorite client stories is this one younger Asian gentlemen. He was newly out of the closet, not too much dating experience. Still living with his parents because in that culture, you did not leave the coup unless you had a significant other prompting you to leave the roost. He came to us looking homeless (this is quite the exaggeration), and through some gentle coaching in wardrobe, his transformation was jaw-dropping. By no means was I trying to change him, but I wanted people to see the immediate kindness and professionalism I saw through his clothing. He felt like a new man too, and that was my goal. I checked in with him one time and he said, "So-and-I are still together, enjoying life and sharing experiences. A relationship is not easy, but it is definitely good to have someone you can share your every day with and explore happiness together." I can die happy knowing that I propelled this transformation in this one individual. His life has been changed forever.

Keepers get married to keepers. Keepers make the time to communicate to their partner each and every day. Keepers find the joy in their partner every day. Keepers put their career *after* their partner. Keepers keep referring to their past as "Been there, done that, already got that out of my system." Keepers place sex on the lower rung of their relationship totem pole. Intimacy trumps the purely physical. Keepers find their partner sexy as hell. Keepers love unconditionally.

I love when people say, "I've read your articles, and I am not that person." Funny thing is that you don't have to prove anything to me. Your actions decide that inclination with someone even before a word comes out of your mouth. I can't tell you how many people conduct themselves one way in our initial interviews and are surprisingly Mr. Casanova on dates. Be cognizant of what you are saying, without you even making an audible sound. I can't remind everyone enough of that. You are in the world of gay men, where first impressions are huge and easily permanent. Men can indulge me with proverbial bacon, but think of me as a strict vegetarian, and that doesn't do it for me. I need emotional bacon, the actions and words that nourish my soul and allow me to perpetuate a bond I feel is mutually understood.

Step One: Love Yourself

I look back at my life in the past couple of years and realize how much I love who I am. This took a bit of soul-searching, but I finally am able to say what I can and can't do in regard to relationships and professional endeavors. This doesn't necessarily come from a conceited point of view but one of self-identification. I know I am an amazing communicator, and with that, being clear and transparent in what I am looking for in a partner. I can come off a little too strong, and I realize this. I just know what I like and what I don't, so I go for it wholeheartedly if the universe is telling me to voice my admiration in the most natural way possible. I am not saying to shack up right away but to enjoy the process in getting to know someone. Relationships develop over months of opportunities to develop lasting, heartfelt moments that turn into loving ones. In turn, I also realized that I can be hard to read. I could care less about things that stem from surface flattery. I need sustenance to feed my soul. I am now drawn to someone's clockwork, drive, and cerebral honesty. Maybe it was me thinking the commercialized version of what the perfect boyfriend meant to me. Hello, real world, and having more humanistic expectations. For me, the notorious men that fall through the cracks have been quickly targeted and disposed. They have always faded naturally to black in the wings of the stage I wish to shine on.

I went through most of my twenties viewing through a telescope of the majority, when really I should have been using a periscope the entire time. When I say I wanted someone who was just "normal," that indication was actually of a minority. The majority can be a bit abnormal in what we are really searching for in a solid connection. It's abnormal for someone to be going out at bars over four or five times a week (or at least people who have responsible career endeavors). It's abnormal to spend multiple hours a day on the phone trying to find a *tonight* or a slim possibility of a responsible date. It's abnormal to attempt to make a true human connection on a dating app that will only give you seconds before the word *next* is abruptly muttered. My manta has been to turn the gay culture into a conversation culture rather from a hookup culture. If I wanted to be a majority, I would do the things that everyone else was doing, and I should expect the same results. I am a true believer in the value of time. That is probably one of my top preferences when I am actively dating. None of my friends cancel or flake last minute, and as you know, we always plan in advance for things. I know I am going into very uncomfortable territory when a guy cancels a date three hours before we are to meet on a brunch date because he had "too many" the night before. I'm sorry, I am too old to deal with your juvenile shenanigans. You should care how people view your time. Notice how responsible and accountable your punctual friends are versus the ones that are always "running behind schedule."

Think of it this way. You get what you pay for. Would I rather pay for a pair of cheap shoes from a name brand commercial retailer and have them fall apart in a matter of months or invest in a good pair and have them last a lot longer, get a little dirt on them, and learn and feel a thing or two from the journey? It's important to shop smart. Everyone wants a quick fix. The thing about quick fixes is that they are instantaneous and sometimes immature, and in the end, we always regret not buying the more expensive pair initially. As a reminder, we can be our own worst enemy as gay men. Where has the hope gone to as a gay community? Why must we dilute our character to satiate a culture that is on an oily surface?

I was at the gym one day, and here approaches a blind man making his way from machine to machine. I was at a shoulder press machine and was so overcome with emotion that I couldn't finish my last set. I sat there in awe and started to cry. I was so inspired by this man, and it made me realize that as humans, we spend a lot of our lives making excuses, which takes more energy than actually reaching our goals themselves. He was there merely because of drive and determination without seeking what most people want from a gym: vanity, something he couldn't physically see from the exterior. This man not only was fighting a physical handicap but seeing him fight as he was working himself to optimal physical exertion was overwhelmingly inspiring. This representation of true vigor had me touched to the point of emotional perseverance. It changed me, just in a matter of minutes. Thank you, whoever you are.

I also had someone mention to me about showing up. Meaning, you creating the stage for your life and how you want your show to be run. By letting people devalue you, you're giving them permission to hinder the experience of your show. I am a firm believer in energy and how it can manifest itself in ways that are mostly understated or go ignored for too long. By allowing those people who consistently provide you with experiences that are insulting or not up to par, they are disrespecting your integrity. They are not living your truth but asking you to live theirs, which is lowering your bar of potential. Don't settle for anything more than what you feel you deserve on an achievable scale. Build a strong stage of character and fire the novice and irresponsible that damaged your spotlight.

When you find the love of your life, you want someone who challenges you and who supports your growth as a person and even makes you a better partner. Only being with someone for the sake of complacency is cheapening the zest life has to offer you. Life is too short and precious to be going through it with your head down rather than seeing what the world has to offer right in front of you. Being complacent is where relationships start to falter and fail. It's our opportunity as quality gay men to not be a statistic anymore but a form of inspiration for our younger gay brothers. We aren't the slutty, drug-induced party animals that society sees us as anymore. We have overcome a lot, especially with the accomplishment of marriage equality on a nationwide scale. It's now our purpose as a community to love ourselves enough to realize that those forms of judgment do not serve us but serves a demeaning cliché. Sometimes we must veer to the left at the fork in the road when the easy way out is toward the right, where the majority is following suit.

I have finally woken up, and the smell of coffee is pungent, in a very real way. For years, I would be told that I was too thin, asked if I was okay, or if I was feeling well. Geez, I had lost fifty pounds, and people were just freaking out. For me, I was tired of complacency. I was tired of eating my mostly vegetarian granola diet. I loved the idea of challenging myself not just to get a hot summer bod but just the motivation and internal discipline that it created within me. I was okay with that piece more than any other.

Dating in general is one treacherous beast. There were times that I loved being single and spent that time focusing on deepening friendships when they needed me the most from life's confines of tragedy. I spent a lot of time weeding out all the "convenient" relationships in my life. You know, the people that are only your friend when it's convenient for them. I have many friends at this point in my life that love and care for me through and through. I need to value, focus, and admire those rather than being in social circles that deem me more popular. In dating, there were times where I was just frustrated and was too quick to judge people and just plainly blew it. There were times where I wanted to date, but my dating well was so harrowing and dry. There were times that I just didn't know what I wanted. There were times that someone misled me and hurt me. There were also times where I was trying to date many people at once and failed miserably, or it was a damn good success. There were times where I just needed a one-night stand. There were times where my heart was severely broken, and I wanted to shrivel up in a corner and weep, and there were times where I felt weightless because of the amount of genuine connection and love I was experiencing.

I found that over the years, I am starting to realize that a person's friends tell me a lot of who they are. It's something I have alluded to before, and it now has worked itself in my personal search as one of my top qualities I look for in an ideal mate. You are what you eat, and whom you eat with says a lot about you. I have friends that spend a lot of their days going out with the same people but would never think about calling them in an emergency. The label "friend" can be so contrived and readily thrown nowadays. At the end of the day, we need to start defining what that is versus an acquaintance.

A lot of gay men seem to have the same friends who all look the same, have the same interests, and communicate the same way. I've had birthdays in the past where people would comment about how my friends are always very different from one another, a bit of a hodgepodge. It's kind of like being a part of the Land of Misfit Toys, but in the best way possible. I've always been attracted to unique things that might be labeled as weird. I love hearing those facts in dating profiles too—they always make you stand out from a rather conventional and mainstream crowd. The unexpected gives us intrigue, and that intrigue becomes mysterious and sometimes fascinating to us. This can attribute to a billowing sense of attraction. As an adolescent, I was the drama kid who would go to the football games in the bus with the band kids, be the editor of the yearbook, would take score at the volleyball games, and would be a part of the anime club. In this sense, no one gets ahead by being complacent and going with the grain all the time. Through those processes, it wasn't a matter of me putting tabs on myself to seem greater to other people but the fact that it made me feel internally better to be exposed to many areas that challenged me and allowed me to grow. I am a very results-oriented and pragmatic fella. I am not impressed by the amount of people "you know who can help me." No, I do not want to see your comedy show, go to your nonprofit event, or fill a seat during your city council meeting, because you have not shared the same interest in supporting my endeavors. If I do not attend, this isn't a reflection on my character or disinterest; this is about how I feel close to you as a friend and not an acquaintance. There are certain expectations that come with both labels, and I am one to not get offended easily. People will forever follow through with things they deem as important. We as a busy species don't have all this ample free time just to go somewhere. Everything must be done with a solidified plan and purpose.

One of my mentors had posted a video blog about creating successful relationships via networking. This can be applied to both business and personal relationships. Why don't you ask me first to see if I am a good fit for your referral as opposed to sending me someone I may not even need or could help in the long-term. This could also easily be said about dating. That's why your personal friends who deeply care about you are your secret weapons. I'll always remember a friend of mine interrupting a video call with a person I was dating at that time and blurting, "Do you want a relationship? Mason doesn't want his time wasted." That could seem rude to a lot of people, but I actually liked the satirical exchange. He was pushy for me but had some realism in a playfully sarcastic way. Let your true friends be picky for you, and trust that they can be one of your best in-person filters. I will always advocate that this is one of the most successful ways to create an amazing first date opportunity.

July 12, 2014, has a special place in my heart. I'm not the weird hippy dippy spiritual type, but every once in a while, I get a vivid premonition of the future. As I was getting a massage that day, I experienced one that was so vivid that I started to cry. Thank goodness I had a towel over my eyes to hide my embarrassment! I remember being in a large open room with hardwood floors, with large windows, with a view of a city. I also remember seeing white lilies, because they were my favorite. This was my home, and I wasn't in LA. I was wearing a long Barney purple V-neck sweater with dark jeans, and I was with my lover, who was taller than me, Caucasian, and had brown hair. I was older, probably ten years from now, because I remember seeing gray in the sides of my sideburns. I remember being held and remember feeling really loved and safe. Whoa.

My challenge to you is to try to think things differently. Try to see the act of desire as an act of achievement itself without expecting any sort of outcome. We go through our life chasing a dream without even realizing the pace we chose to get there. Take initiative and be dynamically innovative. Be a man of your word. Be honest, even though it could mean losing someone, but in that process, you'll never lose yourself. Be a man who is aware that his internal work can almost be his best friend and best filter to bringing the man of his dreams right to his doorstep.

Be brave. Take a leap. Be the strongest version of yourself.

About the Author

Mason R. Glenn is a young aspiring author that offers an astute perspective to true connection in the full spectrum of a gay man. Mason has been consistently inspired and intrigued by the thought process of gay men in their date practices. As a professional matchmaker, for many years, Mason has been able to transform the lives of individuals to feel the full capacity of unconditional love. Intuition has been his gift, and he gathers that through the study of the human mind and collecting quantitative and qualitative data from his professional experiences. There's always some involvement of some street-smarts too, and Mason is able to create a comprehensive dating plan that creates transformational success from all these variables collectively. Mason continues to write and work with matchmaking companies as an expert in the gay male demographic. Mason also leads seminars that hopefully resonates as a gayme changer for the individuals who wish to seek something that will make them better gay men for themselves, their loved ones, and their fellow community.

CPSIA information can be obtained
at www.ICGtesting.com
Printed in the USA
FSOW01n0634200117
29808FS